Long Way Down
THE ILLUSTRATED EDITION

Also by Ewan McGregor and Charley Boorman

Long Way Round
Long Way Round: The Illustrated Edition
Long Way Down

By Charley Boorman
Race to Dakar

Long Way Round and *Long Way Down* are
also available as audiobooks from Hachette Digital

Long Way Down
THE ILLUSTRATED EDITION

Ewan McGregor and Charley Boorman

with Jeff Gulvin

Abridged by Kati Nicholl

sphere

For Olivia, Doone and Kinvara for being there for me.
I love you always.

CHARLEY BOORMAN

For Sheila, who loved the tales of our first trip; for Lou,
who I wish I could tell the stories of this one, and for
Eve and the girls, who I rode every mile to get home to.

EWAN McGREGOR

SPHERE

First published in Great Britain in 2008 by Sphere

Copyright © Long Way Down Ltd, 2008

The moral right of the authors has been asserted.

A CIP catalogue record for this book
is available from the British Library.

ISBN 978-1-84744-249-9

Printed and bound in Germany

Sphere
An imprint of
Little, Brown Book Group
100 Victoria Embankment
London EC4Y 0DY

An Hachette Livre UK Company
www.hachettelivre.co.uk

www.littlebrown.co.uk

CONTENTS

PROLOGUE   8

1 THE BEGINNING   10

2 SADDLE BAGS & SCRAPES   16

3 FIVE . . . FOUR . . . THREE   22

4 HERE WE GO, CHARLEY   34

5 COBBLESTONES, CARS AND KISSING   42

6 UNDER AFRICAN SKIES   50

7 HERE'S SAND IN YOUR EYE!   60

8 ICE COLD IN ALEX   74

9 PYRAMIDS & PORN   84

10 RIDING BIKES & SAVING LIVES   94

11 THE STUFF OF DREAMS   104

12 THE SAND IN SUDAN   114

13 KALASHNIKOVS & CUSTOMS   128

14 A CUP OF GINGER TEA   136

15 THE ROAD AT THE END OF THE WORLD   148

16 SAND, SORROW & CEREMONY   168

17 SIZE DOES MATTER   198

18 ANOTHER COUNTRY   212

19 DESTINATION: 'TRANSIT'   222

20 LILONGWE DOWN   232

21 OUT IN THE CUDS WITH THE GIRLS   242

22 A MOTORCYCLE DIARY   260

APPENDIX A ROUTE   280

APPENDIX B EQUIPMENT   282

PICTURE CREDITS   284

SO WHAT NEXT?   285

ACKNOWLEDGEMENTS   287

PROLOGUE

EWAN: I said goodbye to Charley and left the workshop. It was a Friday afternoon in February and we were heading out with our families for a joint skiing trip the next morning. We were looking forward to the break: things had been hectic lately with preparations for our Africa trip really beginning in earnest.

I was on my BSA Lightning, the roads choked with rush hour traffic. I've lived in London for years, though, and I'm well used to it. It's only traffic, after all; it isn't sand or deep gravel; it's not 'The Road of Bones'.

Charley and I had crossed Kazakhstan on our motorbikes, we'd negotiated the wilderness of Siberia. I'd ridden round the world and now I was really looking forward to riding again with Charley. The two of us riding through Africa, relying on each other.

The traffic was at a standstill. I was filtering up to the lights thinking about my wife Eve and watching my three gorgeous daughters learning to ski.

Suddenly a pedestrian stepped between the vehicles right in front of me.

Brakes on, I was into a skid and shouting, 'Watch out!'

But he didn't see me.

I had no choice but to throw the bike away from him. I was off, chucking the machine to my right, flying through the air. I clattered into him and he was down but at least the bike hadn't hit him. I was still flailing forwards, the road coming up with sickening speed and the bike still revving above me.

Eve and the kids waiting for me at home. Charley and the team – everything we'd planned together.

My body slammed into the road. Was it all over before we'd even begun?

'The adventure was on again – John O'Groats to Cape Town:
we would ride the Long Way Down.' EWAN

1

THE BEGINNING

CHARLEY: It started in October 2004, very late one Friday night in the office in Bulwer Street. This is where Long Way Round had begun, where we'd planned everything, checked and re-checked the maps, it's where we'd first seen the bikes.

It was over, finished: we'd ridden around the world, an epic adventure. But the maps were still on the wall and we stood before them once more. Ewan glanced at me.

'What do you reckon, Charley?'

I looked at him. 'What about riding through Africa?'

Ewan and I first met on a film set in County Clare more than a dozen years ago, our friendship born out of our passion for motorbikes. We've been best mates ever since. We'd always talked about riding together; France maybe, Spain. But then we decided we'd go the whole hog and ride around the world, the adventure of a lifetime that proved to be a pivotal point in my life.

I grew up in the movie business, but after Long Way Round the direction of my life altered. I found myself in places like the pit lane of Moto GP circuits with heroes like Kenny Roberts grabbing my arm and telling me how much he'd enjoyed watching our journey.

I was no longer just John Boorman's son – in fact my dad rang me up the other day to tell me he'd introduced himself to someone and they'd said, 'Oh, Charley Boorman's dad'.

My career was now in motorcycling and together with Russ Malkin, a very good friend and producer/director of *Long Way Round*, I entered the world's most dangerous race: the 2006 Dakar rally – five days in January where I rode ridiculous distances at ridiculous speeds before an innocuous crash tipped me off and I broke both my hands.

Ewan flew in for the end of the Dakar to congratulate us all (my team mate Simon Pavey made it all the way to the finishing line). Ewan was joined by film maker David Alexanian, the fourth member of the team that created *Long Way Round*. There we were in Dakar – all together again. And there in the scorching sun we confirmed what we had first mapped out over a year before in Bulwer Street. The adventure was on again – John O'Groats to Cape Town: we would ride the Long Way Down.

JOHN O

Once my hands were healed, the first thing Ewan and I did was return to the Royal Geographical Society in London, where we'd mapped out the first trip. In the journey-planning office we met the same assistant we'd spoken to before and she had yet more large-scale maps spread on a mahogany table.

She smiled a little warily. 'There are security issues.'

She was right; we'd need armed guards to get us through places like northern Kenya. This was going to be a very different journey from Long Way Round.

From the Royal Geographical Society we headed for the wilds of Devon and a survival course. The weather was shit, a cold, drizzling rain, and to make things even more miserable, Ewan had his tent up before me. He was crowing about it. I mean, he never gets his tent up before me. It was galling.

After that we got lost in the 'wild wood' whilst hunting for strategically placed survival rations, and then we had to build shelters from fallen branches and bits of foliage.

Not that we're competitive or anything, but my A-frame and ridge was up whilst Ewan was still going on about the 'bell end' being big enough.

Lying inside my feet stuck out, though I only discovered that when the instructor kicked them. He proceeded to tell us about a friend of his who went to sleep with his head sticking out of a similar shelter in Africa, only to be woken by a hyena ripping off his face. Our instructor liked telling those kinds of stories a lot.

Ewan was still arranging leaves and ferns. 'Colour coding confuses your enemy,' I heard him mutter.

Finally he was finished and stretched out inside. The instructor asked him if he felt confident that it was structurally sound.

Ewan replied that he did.

'Good,' the instructor said, 'because I'm going to walk on it.'

He'd barely shifted his weight when the 'bell end' Ewan had been so proud of collapsed, showering our Jedi Knight in broken branches.

EWAN: The instructor really did like his tales of horror: hyenas eating people; the machete-wielding madmen lurking outside every bar. Having said that, he also told us that despite our laid-back attitude, I was 'wily' and Charley was really 'industrious'.

From Devon, hyenas and elephants, it was Essex and a replica of the border between the Democratic Republic of Congo and Rwanda. Driving down a track in a 4x4 we were ambushed – a mine exploded in front of the truck.

David Alexanian, who would be joining us on the real trip, was driving. He immediately started backing up. More flash bangs went off behind us.

Now we heard the rattle of gunfire and a man appeared on our right, wearing camouflage and carrying an AK-47. We dived for the doors on the passenger side only to find another guy bellowing and brandishing vicious-looking axes.

We piled out of the vehicle. Hands in the air, we tried to talk to the gunmen – a whole gang of them now. We tried to explain about UNICEF, and what we were doing. They weren't listening. We were forced away from the vehicles, our captors demanding money, jackets, watches, jewellery.

Planning the route started back in January 2007, at our Avonmore Road office.

We'd discussed such a situation with our instructors. Our trip was high profile and we knew we were potential targets. Charley and I had decided that if we were attacked we'd try to get the hell out of there and double back to the last town we'd been through to raise the alarm.

During the exercise however, with explosions and gunfire, we had no time to do anything except put our hands above our heads.

CHARLEY: We returned to London with an even stronger sense of the dangers we would be facing on the trip. But little did we know that the first accident would take place not at some remote African border, but on a busy street in west London. And it could put the whole trip in jeopardy.

' Our route was down through Britain and France to the toe of Italy and across Sicily before a boat ride to Tunisia. Once in Africa we would follow the coast to Libya, Egypt and Sudan. ' CHARLEY

2

LONDON

SADDLE BAGS & SCRAPES

EWAN: I sprawled on my face and the bike came slamming full force right into my leg.

For a moment I just lay there, looking up at this guy who was looking down at me with his eyes popping out of his head.

'Jesus,' I said. 'Are you all right?'

'Yeah, I'm fine.' Still he stood there gawping. He was in shock. I was in shock.

Then another guy arrived and picked the bike off my leg. I staggered to my feet but as I did so I felt something go and a sickening sensation worked through me. I hobbled off the road and sat down.

The bloke got my bike to the pavement and I took off my boot. My leg was burning. I'd grazed it quite badly and I could feel a weird sensation just above the ankle.

Finally the man I'd hit seemed to come to, and he walked over and asked me if I was all right.

'I think I might've broken my ankle.'

'No, you couldn't have broken it. You wouldn't be able to walk on it, would you? Not if it was broken.'

For a moment my spirits lifted. 'No,' I said. 'You're right.'

A policewoman arrived on a horse. Or at least I think she did because the whole thing felt surreal.

She asked if everyone was OK.

The guy I'd hit was apologising, telling me he'd been looking the other way.

'Look,' I said, 'so long as you're OK. I'm fine.' I was just delighted he hadn't been hurt.

They talked about calling for an ambulance. But all I wanted was to get home. If I could stand, I could ride, and pulling on my boot I grabbed my helmet and gloves.

All at once I was hobbling across the pavement with this weird clicking sensation in my leg.

The right hand foot peg was buckled to being vertical, which made it useless but with hindsight it was actually a blessing. It meant I could get my foot fully under the gear shift so I could change gear without having to flex my ankle.

Somehow I got the bike kick-started. I managed to nudge it into first and then I was in the traffic and completely focused on getting home. Nothing else mattered. Every time I stopped, however, I had to put my foot down. That hurt like hell and I thought: fuck, this is bad.

When Eve opened the door I could see the concern in her face as I hovered there, half-balanced on one foot.

'Ewan, my God! What happened?'

'I crashed, Eve. I think I need my leg X-rayed.'

In the car I felt my ankle and there didn't seem to be any real swelling. But then I noticed a little lump pressing the skin on the back of my calf. I pushed it and a wave of panic washed over me. I could feel it move, a hideous sensation of bone moving over bone – the fibula was snapped.

I could've cried.

My leg was broken and one by one the implications began to hit. There was the skiing trip and a month from now I was due on the set of a film. Fucking hell: Long Way Down, we were leaving on motorbikes for Africa on 12 May. All the hard work, the massive amount of organisation and here I was, en route to hospital.

CHARLEY: Ewan phoned and told me what had happened.

'Fuck it,' he said bitterly. 'I saw the X-ray. Clear as day, snapped above the ankle.'

All sorts of thoughts began racing through my head; first and foremost concern for my friend, then the ski trip, and of course Long Way Down.

'Did the nurse tell you how long it would take to heal?'

'Four to six weeks.'

'Then we're OK. Don't worry about it. It's just one of those things.'

'That's what I thought.' I could hear the relief in Ewan's voice. 'It's plenty of time. It just means I can't go skiing which is a real pain for Eve and the kids.'

When I put the phone down, it started sinking in how lucky he'd been – and the other guy. Hitting a pedestrian – it was scary, a warning. Our biggest concern about riding bikes in Africa was hitting someone. When we rode round the world we went through some serious country but often it was remote and the terrain was the challenge. Africa was a whole different ball game. In Africa roads are the lifeblood, the arteries that feed the continent and they're very busy. Hitting someone was our worst nightmare.

Vividly I recalled snapping my collarbone not long before we were due at the Dakar. And the scaphoid, the most important bone in my wrist, dislocated, not to mention shattered knuckles in my other hand. Just as Ewan had ridden home with a busted leg, I picked the bike up and carried on. I'd had no choice and no idea how bad my injuries were. In the end I rode another four hundred and fifty kilometres.

Olly, my beautiful wife, is the rock that holds my life together. She puts up with me; she looks after the kids while I take off and at the same time she runs a business called Share and Care with her sister-in-law Caroline. She deals with everything, takes it all in her stride and never complains about anything. Olly knew what was going through my mind. 'It puts things in perspective, doesn't it?' she said. 'I mean, don't get me wrong, the trip is wonderful, it's very exciting. But it's much more dangerous, and not just the politics. The roads are busier and there are people everywhere.' She shook her head. 'It just shows how lucky the two of you were when you did Long Way Round, Charley. Twenty thousand miles with no major incident.'

EWAN: Departure was just days away now. The cast was off my leg and the bikes were prepped. Russ and David were up to their necks trying to finalise everything.

When we prepared for Long Way Round, the support trucks didn't show up until the day before we left. Here we still had a day or so and both Nissan Patrols were ready. We had a team of people coming to the workshop on Avonmore Road to fit a safe and some bullet cameras. The small, fixed 'bullet' cameras made by Sonic would be fitted in the Nissans and on our helmets and would allow the action to be filmed at all times. The suspension had been upgraded and both trucks fitted with dual batteries; they had long-range fuel tanks and two spare wheels apiece. The front bumpers had been replaced with ones that carried a winch in case Russ or David had to haul themselves out of a hole somewhere.

CHARLEY: The bikes had been painted blue and red for Ewan and I respectively. We'd fitted sump guards and light guards; metal protection plates over the engine casing. We'd also switched the original BMW suspension for what was considered the more robust Ohlins. We changed the weightier exhausts for Akrapovic cans, which were not only lighter but added around four or five horsepower. MacTools had provided all the necessary tools and Touratech had supplied all the gear we'd need, from tents to camping stoves to mounts for our mobile phones. We had Nokia's Navigator 6110, both communication and navigation that we could use all the way through Africa and supplied by AST we had satellite equipment so we could send footage back to the office.

Our route was down through Britain and France to the toe of Italy and across Sicily before a boat ride to Tunisia. Once in Africa we would follow the coast to Libya, Egypt and Sudan. We'd always known Libya might be an issue and we were encountering problems getting visas for the two Americans on our team: David Alexanian and cameraman Jimmy Simak. We'd only just got the requisite paperwork for the Brits and Claudio, the Swiss cameraman who had also ridden with us on Long Way Round.

Then Friday came and we left for Scotland.

'The scenery was stunning: mountains banked with heather and massive stands of firs. The way they smelled in the rain was terrific. I was getting hungry and thinking about scampi and chips. What is it about road trips through Scotland that make you think about eating scampi and chips?' EWAN

3

SCOTLAND

FIVE ... FOUR ... THREE

EWAN: The Castle of Mey, the historic seat of the Earls of Caithness. Built in the sixteenth century, the castle is said to be haunted by a daughter of the fifth earl. But I had a really good night's sleep.

My dad and brother Colin were riding through Scotland with us and I was really pleased about that. My leg was much better. But over breakfast I began to feel apprehensive, my nerves were beginning to bite.

The trucks were packed, the bikes ready, and we were all set. I pulled up alongside Charley. 'OK, Charley,' I said. 'Good luck, mate. Love you.'

The sign read 'John O'Groats, a welcome at the end of the road' but for us it was the beginning and quite a few people had gathered to see us off.

I told Charley I really had to speak to my wife. 'I haven't told her I'm leaving yet.'

He was laughing. 'You mean you've not told her we're doing the trip?'

'No, I just said I was going out to get some milk.'

I spoke to Eve, the whole gathering yelling out 'hello'. And then we were off – myself, Charley, my dad, my brother, and Claudio filming on the camera bike.

I love riding motorcycles. It can be raining, snowing, I don't care. There's no feeling quite like it in the world, the bike sweeping into bends, banking the thing knowing it's planted, no matter the road conditions. And when you're riding there's so much time to reflect, which is a rare thing these days.

John O'Groats was the perfect place to start. A couple of days in beautiful Scotland was good for the soul. I was relaxed, the Belstaff rally suit was light, comfortable and, most important, waterproof. I was in my element.

CHARLEY: We were heading down the A9 towards Loch Ness before riding through Glencoe and on to Crieff.

Cape Town was months and a hell of a lot of miles away. There'd been a kidnapping in Ethiopia, plane crashes in the Congo, and the situation in Darfur was no better. There'd been a rally in London to protest about the four years of slaughter and we weren't sure what impact that would have on the Sudanese government.

I guessed we'd find out.

It was beginning to rain. We headed south, a loch on our left and the mountains sombre and grey. Ewan was right, Scotland had been a good idea; the roads were empty, the bike felt like it was on rails and to be riding with my best mate again was fantastic.

Beyond the black waters of Loch Ness we headed east through Glencoe. Here the mountains shouldered us on either side and Ewan described the history as 'bleeding off them'.

EWAN: The scenery was stunning: mountains banked with heather and massive stands of firs. The way they smelled in the rain was terrific. I was getting hungry and thinking about scampi and chips. What is it about road trips through Scotland that make you think about eating scampi and chips?

We spent the night with my mum in Crieff and in the morning we headed for Stirling and then Robin House. Only the second children's hospice to be built in Scotland, it's a place where parents can take their terminally ill youngsters and get a little respite themselves. It's run by the Children's Hospice Association of Scotland, a charity I'm involved with. I'd not been to Robin House since it was completed, but I had been to its sister Rachel House in Kinross. The best way to describe the children is as wonderfully brave little people who aren't going to make it into adulthood. They're feisty, full of life; they're very much alive. How do you deal with it though ... if you're a parent, I mean? I think unless you're actually in it, it's unimaginable.

Robin House is set within the boundaries of Loch Lomond National Park. We pulled up and were met by the staff; inside one of the kids was hovering. I gave him a big hug. 'Hi, wee man,' I said. 'How are you?'

CHARLEY: For years Ewan had been telling me about CHAS and what fantastic work they did, how incredible the families involved were. But until today I'd never seen for myself. I have to admit I was feeling quite emotional. I spoke to Ewan in the spacious reception area. I said that as well as it being so hard on the children and parents, it must be really tough for the staff.

Ewan nodded. 'What you find being here though ... it's a really positive experience because it's a place full of life. I've always found it at Rachel House. That's what it's for, for these kids to have a really good time. And so you come away feeling really good.'

It was an incredible building, wood-panelled with windows everywhere. The views across the gardens to the distant hills were magnificent. The staff took us into the sitting room where families were gathered and they'd put a big sign on the wall welcoming us. There was the usual hubbub, music in the background, loud and crashy, not even vaguely melancholy. We met a great lad called William who'd come all the way from Rachel House especially because his greatest ambition had been to meet Ewan. There was a lad called Sean from Stirling, a young lady called Ashleigh, there was Cameron, Keiron, Lee; and a little girl called Rebecca who was running around taking everyone's picture. Outside a wheelchair-bound boy named Paul was flying a kite with one of the carers, while someone's younger brother dressed as Superman dived about all over the place.

The parents had bedrooms downstairs – an escape zone so they could get away from it all for a while. The families, brothers and sisters particularly, take advantage of the pool because with one child needing constant care they rarely go to a normal swimming pool. The kids have a main play area complete with a soft play room, where those who can't stand up are able to roll around without getting hurt. They have a fantastic art room where the music is so loud you can barely hear yourselves speak.

With the children, parents and staff at Rachel House: it was a day we'd never forget.

A lot of the kids they deal with are teenagers. They have their own den, where no adult or young child can go; a chill-out zone where they can surf the net, watch DVDs or play the drums if they want to. The hospice has what they call the snoozlin: a multi-sensory area with coloured bubble lights, a water bed, a carpet that changes colour and a ceiling made of stars. Children who can't communicate can lie there and perhaps some image or colour will bring a light to their eyes or even the hint of a smile.

Most of the time I was fighting back tears. We met a girl called Jenna whose dad was a biker, another girl called Jenny, there was Leona and John; I'd never come across such brave children or such incredible parents. The whole thing was humbling and left Ewan and me feeling very emotional, particularly after they showed us the rainbow room.

The hospice is there to create memories for families who are losing their children. That's what they told us, and it was a terribly sad and yet kind of hopeful way of putting it. For me it was personified in the rainbow room: it looked like any other bedroom but this was where a child was laid out after he or she had died. It was private and separate and could be made very cool very quickly so a grieving family could have as long as they wanted with their loved one. They could play music or read a story, or they could just sit with them until they could face moving on. If they woke in the night in floods of tears they could go to the rainbow room and just be with them.

The carers told us that ironically the room comes to life when a child is lying there; they have hidden projectors and can play images across the walls, photos would be spread, memories. If the child was just a baby, perhaps only a few days old, ceramic imprints of their hands and feet can be made. They told us about a weekend they had when one of the kids died and all the others went to the rainbow room to say goodbye. Talk about tough, talk about brave; they knew this was what faced every one of them.

It made me think about my sister Telsche, who I lost to cancer eleven years ago. I missed her. I loved her. I could feel her with me on the bike, almost as if when I slung my leg over the seat she climbed right on the back. She was there on Long Way Round; she was there on the Dakar. I knew she'd be with me all the way to Cape Town.

EWAN: I've visited Rachel House many times and it puts everything into the sharpest focus. You just have to thank God that places like Robin House are there, because for the families that use them they're an absolute necessity, and the carers, the people that work there, can't be praised enough.

We reluctantly said our goodbyes and rode on to Erskine Hospital, an establishment for ex-service people that my brother is involved with. We spoke to some ex-soldiers – one old boy in particular had been part of the actual Great Escape. Then Charley spoke to a bloke who'd served with Robert Lawrence, a friend of Charley's who had been horrifically wounded in the Falklands. He wrote about his experiences in the controversial book *Tumbledown*.

It had been an incredible, inspiring day. In their different ways both places had taught us something about the nature of courage and it was a privilege to have been invited.

My dad left us now. He'd loved riding with us and I'd loved having him there. But he was heading home and we were going to Cape Town. We shed tears and parted company and then there were four bikes on the road.

We cut across country, south-east to the desolate location of Holy Isle. It's built on a promontory beyond a causeway which floods at high tide, and the wind howls in an almost permanent gale. But there was a barren beauty to it even so.

A little further on a couple of people came rushing out of their house, waving their arms. I pulled up. They told me that they'd been following our departure on a website. Dave and Claire, both BMW riders: I told them to get the kettle on. They were the first of many along the route who would show us great hospitality – and this was half the fun of the trip for me.

My brother was heading back to Edinburgh in the morning. And then the four would become three. We rode south and on the third night camped at Silverstone – by the bend before the start and finish straight. Apparently we were the first people in the racetrack's sixty year history to actually camp there.

It was the ideal opportunity to test the stuff. My tent was great; dry and cosy and plenty big enough for me and all my gear. It rained in the night but when I packed up everything was bone dry.

Before we left Charley and I followed a pace car for two laps of the track with the Nissan Patrols following. It was pouring with rain, but still Charley managed a second gear wheelie.

From Silverstone it was on to London, the Avonmore Road workshop, the gang, and home for one last night with our families.

'My heart was pounding, adrenalin pumping and I was sweating buckets. I concentrated. I had to: my pulse was racing so much I was in danger of crashing.' EWAN

4

LONDON & ITALY

HERE WE GO, CHARLEY

The Long Way Down team gave us a fantastic send off.

EWAN: The following morning everyone was gathered at Avonmore Road: our families and friends. We said our final goodbyes. Clara, my eldest daughter, was there with my wife, but Esther and Jamyan, my younger two, were at school.

The bikes packed, the trucks ready, we rolled out of the workshop for the last time and everyone was gathered on the pavement. Flags were waved, we had a line painted on the tarmac just as we had before we set off round the world, and we cut a cake made in the shape of a crash helmet.

Shaking hands with Charley, I looked round for my wife. There she was: a smile, a final wave and, pulling my best ever wheelie, I led us off down the road.

My heart was pounding, adrenalin pumping and I was sweating buckets. I concentrated. I had to: my pulse was racing so much I was in danger of crashing - and I'd hit enough pedestrians for one year already.

CHARLEY: Ewan popped the wheelie and I followed him. We were skipping through the traffic when all at once a pickup truck stopped right in front of me. I didn't even see his brake lights. With so much buzzing through my head I wasn't concentrating.

Ten minutes down the road and I'd almost smacked a Mitsubishi up the backside. I had to brake suddenly, the suspension working overtime. Ewan came flashing by on my right.

For a couple of seconds I just sat there, telling myself to chill out. It's what my wife had been telling me – to calm down and enjoy it. Olly always has the right thing to say to me: no matter what angst she might be going through, all she thinks about is how I'm feeling. She's my hero, she really is.

Gradually I relaxed; the traffic eased, we were on the motorway and heading for Folkestone with the Eurostar thundering by on our left.

Two hours later we were boarding the train.

EWAN: We pulled out of the train on the French side of the channel, Charley hoisted the front wheel and I was laughing, excited. France: God it was brilliant; the skies a feathered grey and the road dead straight, just the odd tree to interrupt the horizon.

Oh my God, we're going to Cape Town!

Sitting there on the French motorway I could feel the grin stretching my face.

CHARLEY: Out of the train I pulled a wheelie as I planned to at every border. We were on the continent and heading south and I was totally into the bike.

Ewan had been up for camping tonight but we'd agreed on a hotel outside Reims. The weather looked iffy and we had to get through the Mont Blanc tunnel the following afternoon if we were to make it to the Moto Guzzi factory as planned.

EWAN: In the morning I was glad we'd decided on a hotel because it rained in the night and it was raining now and today was a big push with three hundred and seventy miles to cover.

I was really enjoying myself; I love riding. These trips aren't about getting away from the movie business. They're about melding my two worlds, professional and personal. I love the fact that there aren't a hundred and one people ushering me around like there is when I'm working. Fantastic that no one tells me to get off the motorbike because it's too dangerous and we have to get a stuntman in for those bits. It's partly riding with Charley, of course, partly adventure, and partly just the camaraderie of motorcycling. Everything I need is on that bike: that's why when the opportunity is there to just pull over and put a tent up I want to take it.

The rain was light at first and I was pretty relaxed. Besançon is where Eve's parents have a house; a stunning part of the world, sumptuous countryside, all gorges and rivers, chateaux dotted here and there.

The day wore on and the rain grew heavier. My boots gradually filled with water. Four hours in the sodding rain. My foot was in a spa only the water wasn't hot. *Would somebody get me out of this fucking rain?*

The countryside was dim and grizzled. We were into mountains that on any other day would've been beautiful, but the clouds hung so low all we could see was the swirl of grey and the rain.

We stopped for fuel at a Total garage and I nosed my bike alongside Charley's. 'So, Charley,' I said. 'How do we feel?'

He made a face. 'A bit low actually. Too much sun, a little heatstroke, I think. It's like being on the Dakar.' He glanced at the petrol pump. 'Total sponsored me, actually.'

'Really, Charley?'

'Yeah… Hey, did I ever mention I did the Dakar, Ewan?'

'Yeah, I think you mentioned that. Anyway, it's the dryness of the heat that's the killer.'

'You know somewhere in Africa we'll look back and dream of this day.'

'Somewhere.' With a squelch I shifted position. 'You know what?' I said with a grin.

'What's that?'

I looked up at leaden skies, the rain rattling off our helmets.

'Maybe we'll hotel it tonight.'

CHARLEY: Yeah, we would. I was chilled to the bone and my old bike injuries were hurting me. We rode south, the water lying so deep that now and again we'd aquaplane. I watched the back of Ewan's bike, steady as a rock as he kicked up spray. Riding in the wet is fine; it's a matter of keeping your concentration, keeping the pace up but slowing things down in your mind and making sure everything you do is smooth.

The GPS seemed to have taken on a mind of its own for a moment, telling me it was this way, then that way. I told Ewan and his response was some *Star Wars*-style advice across the radio: 'Trust in the machine, Charley,' he whispered. 'Trust in the machine.'

Wet, I kept thinking. This is fucking wet. The mountains were all but invisible though we were climbing hard now and in and out of tunnels.

I would love to tell you about the spectacular scenery, but I couldn't see it, could I?!

That's how it was, hour after hour. If we weren't in dry tunnels, we were crossing saturated bridges that spanned massive valleys, gorges falling to nothing beneath the wheels. Through a gap in the cloud ahead I could see snow on the Alps.

It's when you stop on a bike that you realise just how cold you are; you start to shiver and shake, especially if you're soaked through. Ewan was in *Star Wars* mode again. 'Charley,' he told me, 'be mindful of your thoughts for they betray you.'

I had no thoughts except getting through the Mont Blanc tunnel, finding the nearest hotel and getting my sodden gear into some kind of drying room.

EWAN: That was the plan, through the tunnel, first hotel and out of the fucking rain. Three hundred and seventy miles and pissing down every inch of the way – but finally we made it: through the toll and out of the rain. Through the tunnel and into Italy – and still it was raining!

CHARLEY: It had been a tough day, but the following morning dawned clear and beautiful. Now we could see the mountains – and our gear was dry.

We were heading across northern Italy towards Lake Como and the sun was high. Green fields, little churches, people working farms, and I could smell the wonderful scent of freshly mown grass. A Ferrari blatted by, very Italian, very chic.

Up ahead Ewan overtook a lorry, a sweet move, and then we were into small towns and the road was great with old buildings pressed up to the kerbs, sand and ochre coloured, and beyond them the mountains shone in the sun.

An hour later our longed-for destination appeared: the Moto Guzzi factory, a series of 1920s buildings carrying the bend in the main street. Painted a sort of amber it looked more like an old hotel than a bike factory.

EWAN: I was in seventh heaven. My first big bike was a Guzzi. I thought it was a 1978 Le Mans when I bought it but it was only pretending. It was some kind of Guzzi, though only the seat and tank had come from a Le Mans. It didn't matter. I loved it and I've been a Guzzi fan ever since.

The factory had plenty of bikes on display; one in particular we just had to sit on, an eight cylinder classic that had won the Isle of Man TT.

Outside they have this amazing test track. It's pretty tight, with the factory squashed in the middle and ivy-covered walls climbing the perimeter. It's four hundred and sixty metres around and the corners are banked. The tester told us he could get up to eighty on it. He had two bikes sitting there and Charley and I jumped on them and did a couple of circuits.

The tester was shaking his head and telling everyone how he really enjoyed his job and would be sad to lose it if one of us happened to peel off.

Russ, David and the trucks had left for Florence but it was still a beautiful day and Charley and I were determined to camp. A few miles from the Guzzi factory we stopped

In heaven at the Moto Guzzi factory.

at a garage and this gentle giant of an Italian used his GPS to find us a campsite. He loaded the coordinates into ours then called the site and booked the three of us in. By seven p.m. we were at the gate.

We rode beyond the camper vans, down to a smaller field that we all but had to ourselves. In no time the tents were up. We had bread and cheese but I wanted something hot and, as I was thinking about it, along came Francine with a pot of pasta.

We'd never seen her before in our lives but here was this redhead with a guy called Walther, and a pot in her hands. She told us they were bikers and they'd been in their van watching us arrive and thought we looked hungry.

It was wonderful, great food just when we needed it and provided by a couple of people from Zurich. It really was moments like these that made the trip so special. We talked about riding motorbikes and explained what we hoped to do. They spoke great English and told us that they had ridden some of the journey themselves. A few years back they'd biked from Cape Town to Dar Es Salaam and we ended up sharing GPS coordinates for campsites in Africa.

'We headed off with olive trees on each side and scooters everywhere; old or young, everyone seemed to ride them.' CHARLEY

ITALY

COBBLESTONES, CARS & KISSING

CHARLEY: Last night had been great, meeting Francine and Walther and sharing the GPS coordinates. It was a new kind of culture, a GPS culture; travellers sharing the coordinates of places. All we had to do was punch the details into our Nokia Navigators and we'd get there. Not like a map. How many times has someone told you about a place you must see and you never get there because you don't write it down properly or can't find it on the map?

I love it, it's great. I'm a gadget guy anyway, but this is about sharing experiences; the beauty of the world witnessed through GPS.

It was another stunning morning in Italy and tonight we'd be in Rome, which was three hundred and fifty miles away, so we couldn't hang about. We headed off with olive trees on each side and scooters everywhere; old or young, everyone seemed to ride them.

We got to Siena before lunch and Ewan pulled up alongside. 'Fantastic, Charley, I love it.'

EWAN: The ride to Siena was brilliant, I was in terrific spirits and it's a great city – ancient yet vibrant, full of life and colour and the architecture is absolutely stunning. And every-where I looked there were classic cars. We chatted to two English guys who had a 1932 Alfa parked up near the square. It turned out the guys were doing the Mille Miglia, a classic road race in pre-1950s cars that went from Brescia to Rome and back to Brescia again.

But for us it was lunch, then back to the bikes and a big stint down to Rome.

CHARLEY: Siena was great and Rome too, but I got up on Sunday morning feeling a bit blah. Too much wine. You know how it is.

We waited while Russ and David sorted the Nissans. Cameraman Jimmy Simak was already perched on the back of David's truck so he could film Ewan and me on the road for a while.

We set off, winding our way through one of the most historic cities in the world. It was hot and slow going; I could hear Ewan whistling though, singing Italian songs, anthems, ice cream adverts. We passed a pyramid. No, I'm serious; a full blown Egyptian pyramid. It reared up out of the trees. It turned out that this was the Pyramid of Cestius, a Roman who decided to be buried Pharoah-style after Rome had conquered Egypt. A fashion thing.

We rode for a while on the Appian Way, the most important road in ancient Rome, stretching from the city to Brindisi down in the south-east. It had been the main thoroughfare for trade and the movement of soldiers. Many of the cobbles were missing now, but that didn't hinder us: up on the foot pegs, Ewan and I rode our bikes along the highway that the Roman Army marched on thousands of years before.

Then it was open roads and two and a half hours to Naples and the Amalfi peninsula. That coast road was stunning: really twisty, the sea on one side, sometimes close by, sometimes hundreds of feet below, with rocks and trees and buildings banked up on the other.

EWAN: The road was fantastic, a biker's paradise, though some of those bends were horrific; one mistake and it would be the last corner you got wrong. The road seemed to be bolted onto the cliff, with houses built in clutches and clinging there like limpets.

When we left Rome I realised that we'd covered more than 2500 miles now. Fantastic! But I barely knew what day it was any more – who the fuck cares?

There were palm trees everywhere, little cobbled streets and orange and yellow buildings with terracotta roof tiles faded by a constant sun. And the people: everyone seemed to be kissing. Every lay-by, couples were snogging. There seemed to be a great deal of love going on in Italy.

South towards Reggio di Calabria it was getting dark and we were tired now. We made the campsite and got the tents up, no longer any competition between us – too weary for that.

The next morning we set off for Palermo; another ten hours of driving, back on the big roads now with the sea on our right as we climbed high, crossing massive bridges with drops that set your hair curling.

From the bridges we'd be in tunnels where the engine note was magnified and lights shone in your face. Charley abreast of me, I waved him on with a smile. I could see the white rag I'd attached to his bike, flapping in the wind. A bit of old T-shirt with Long Way Down on it. The trick was to get it onto his bike unnoticed and see how long it would stay there. It had started on Charley's bike, had been on mine and now it was back with him. Silly games, but fun; it's something we'd done when we rode round the world.

CHARLEY: I knew where it was, I'd get him back, bury it somewhere so I could see it and he couldn't.

We were riding a rugged coastline, with a fort in the distance and Sicily beyond. We made it to the boat; a half hour crossing and we were back in the saddle and gliding down the ramp into the port of Messina with the sun going down in front of us. We burbled through town, stopping and starting; road works, the scene of a recent accident, a reminder of the dangers.

I didn't care though – we were in Sicily and the day after tomorrow we were crossing to Africa.

The next morning I was feeling nervous. I kept thinking about Africa and what could go wrong. Ewan came down and we got the bikes, heading for the BMW dealer to change the tyres to knobblies. As we pulled out from the underground car park this guy and his girlfriend stopped us. He spoke English with an American accent and showed us the way to the BMW dealer.

EWAN: We sat and had a coffee and he explained he was a BMW rider and at four thirty that morning he'd been trawling one of the BMW owners' websites. As you do. He'd been told that Charley and I were in Sicily and he wanted to meet us. He came up with someone who'd seen us arrive at our hotel. They hooked up, two guys who didn't know each other but had BMW trail bikes in common. A few hours later we were all having a coffee.

It was brilliant.

EWAN: It turned out to be a great last day in Europe and in the morning we rode the bikes down to the port at Trapani. The ship was tied off alongside the dock and we were able to ride right up to the open roll-on, roll-off doors.

Russ had all the relevant paperwork ready. It was the first time we'd needed to produce *carnets* for the vehicles and the lists of equipment we were carrying. A little while later we were riding up the ramp – my heart beat faster. Africa was just a boat ride away.

On deck the sea was calm, the crossing ten hours or so and barely a white top to be seen; the sun was shining, it was a beautiful day and we were all together. I could sense a little tension in the air, none of us knew quite what to expect. As Jim Foster had told us, when things kick off in Africa they really kick off, go down hill very quickly and generally there's no warning. Jim was one of our cameramen who'd worked in places like Beirut, Iraq and Afghanistan: he was with us not just to film but to offer a little security should we need it. Forty-five years old, he'd been born in Africa and there wasn't much he couldn't tell us about the politics. He also reminded us that life is cheap and what westerners considered brutality wasn't the same in Africa. It was sobering. We all had our fears and you could sense it now in the atmosphere.

CHARLEY: I could see it now, the Tunisian coast. It was wonderful: Africa finally, almost.

I had the collywobbles. Ewan pointed out what looked like a bunch of windmills, a wind farm; the cliffs were a sandy white and the sea that stunning blue. Beautiful, but it didn't make any difference to how I was feeling.

We'd just had a safety and security briefing: Jim and Dai talked us through the basics of what we had to consider. Dai was our medic; having trained with the army and attached to the SAS, he now worked as a remote access paramedic and, like Jim, he'd served in some serious war zones.

Jim made it clear that unless it was unavoidable we wouldn't be travelling during the hours of darkness; there were too many hazards, trucks without lights, pedestrians, Bosnian motorbikes – as he called the one-eyed monster that's a car with one headlamp out. We all agreed we'd set up a camp spot an hour before darkness.

Before we entered each country we'd have an up-to-date briefing on the situation from London; Jim was very conscious of the changing political landscapes. Again he said how swiftly everything can go pear-shaped; we couldn't leap out of the truck like drama queens (as he put it), cameras pointed, and hope to get away with it. We had to be calm and considered; he and Russ would deal with checkpoints and borders.

Jim reiterated that we'd have to judge every situation on its own merits and to work as a team. A lot of areas in Sudan and Ethiopia were mined; Jim cited a situation with the BBC where the crew jumped out of a truck to film and found themselves in the middle of an unmarked minefield. Explosions started going off. It was a disaster and the poor producer ended up losing a leg.

Going through the medical kit with Dai at the Tunisian border.

We talked through what we'd do in given situations, like if we got separated, robbed or attacked. Jim reminded us that since the British and American governments embarked on their global war on terror, we had to be prepared for people just taking offence regardless of any behaviour on our part.

EWAN: It was still early in the trip and we were finding our feet as a team. I really thought we were gelling; six of us had done this before, Dai and Jim were newcomers, but they were becoming an integral part of the whole. I loved the military banter that passed between them.

I wasn't really nervous, my biggest fear was knocking someone down. But most of all I was excited about the prospect of riding through Africa and as the sun went down we steamed into Tunis. I don't know what I expected, more of a hubbub maybe, noise and bustle, a market scene from an Indiana Jones film, all baskets and snakes and swords.

It was nothing like that – it was a port like any other; quiet really, but it was certainly a border crossing. We docked at half past eight at night but weren't on the road into town until eleven thirty. That was after we'd furnished the customs man with four bottles of vodka. Oh, how it was all coming back to me.

I was excited but relaxed. It was brilliant; the trucks behind, the road clear, tarmac good and lights in the distance. There was a very distinctive smell to the place: a spicy, dusty sort of smell.

'God it was hot. Our first day in Africa and my legs were roasting, the vents in my trousers not creating much airflow. Even sitting in the shade I could feel the sweat sticking to me.' CHARLEY

6

TUNISIA

UNDER AFRICAN SKIES

CHARLEY: Three days later I was in a hotel room in Tripoli squeezing the moisture out of my pillow. It was dark outside and from the balcony I could see kids playing football. In fact there were people everywhere. It was so hot in the daytime, this seemed to be the best time for everyone to congregate in the fresher air.

Downstairs we had our Libyan fixer Nuri, his driver, someone from the ministry of tourism and a guy from the secret police. On top of that some other guy had turned up and we'd no clue who he was. Talk about entourage. The bureaucracy reminded me of Kazakhstan on Long Way Round.

My boots stank: thank heaven this wasn't a scratch and sniff movie or the viewers would be switching channels in droves. I was tired but happy; three days of good riding, a couple of nights camping, and my wife sent me a really lovely text: *I love you and miss you, she said: Try not to worry too much about the unknown. Remember, lots of people have walked, cycled and driven your journey before you, successfully. It's a wonderful, exciting journey you're on. We pray for you every night.*

EWAN: I was thrilled about being in Africa. It was very hot on the road, the tarmac good as we left Tunis. The buildings, white and clean and well spaced, fell away and the highway opened up. Palm trees sprang from the pavements and the central reservation was sand, the verges the same. The sky was vast and empty, a shimmering blue in the heat. We passed a truck overloaded with bolts of cloth flapping in the wind. A pickup stacked with crates stuffed with oranges and lemons: I could hear Charley singing the nursery rhyme through my helmet.

CHARLEY: We pulled into a town for lunch. The buildings were sandstone, mostly single-storey, canopies draped the windows and people waved and smiled as we passed. We found a café, a low wailing music coming from inside. A waiter showed us a rack of lamb's ribs then set to with a massive chopper. He barbecued the meat and we ate it with salads and this really spicy garlic sauce, washed down with bottles of water.

God it was hot. Our first day in Africa and my legs were roasting, the vents in my trousers not creating much airflow. Even sitting in the shade I could feel the sweat sticking to me.

I tucked into the salad and dipped bread in the sauce. We'd been told to avoid salad and washed vegetables because of the water, but I figured we should eat what the locals eat. All the time we were eating a solitary sheep tied to a large pink flowerpot looked on and baaed at us.

'Hey, Charley,' Ewan said. 'There's someone's lunch or dinner right there, or the mother of what we've just eaten, maybe.' He paused then for a moment. 'I'm feeling a little lonely, you know what I mean? Maybe I'll trot over after.'

'Ewan,' I said slowly, 'maybe we ought to leave conversations about sheepage on the cutting room floor.'

After lunch we headed south towards an ancient coliseum at a place called El Jem, some hundred and thirty miles south of the capital.

We discovered an ancient amphitheatre with most of the seats intact. Climbing to the top it was fantastic to gaze across an arena that once had been host to the games and seated up to thirty thousand people.

'Can you imagine the noise, Charley?' Ewan murmured.

We walked down the banks of stone seats and paused before massive ruined arches. We could see the catacombs and passages below ground, where the gladiators would have waited, where the lions were kept together with the poor souls the Romans used to feed to them seventeen hundred years ago.

Back on the bikes we beetled south towards Libya. As it was getting dark we found a place to camp, a clearing surrounded by trees.

In the cuds in Tunisia. Charley was always a dab hand at getting his tent up first.

EWAN: Beyond the trees coarse, prickly bushes drifted to a flattened horizon. I got my tent up, then I gathered wood and set about making a campfire; it was our first since leaving home and it was brilliant. Charley made Bovril drinks to replace some of the salt we'd lost and we cooked dinner with the sun sinking like a fireball, the sky a hazy gold and the trees casting insect-black shadows.

The birds slowly stopped chirping and the sound of cicadas took over. I loved that sound, louder and louder the darker it got.

CHARLEY: The next morning we were on the road early with every vent in our gear open and the jackets all but unzipped. Last night we'd spoken to the others and there was talk of maybe getting to Libya today instead of tomorrow, which was pushing it.

Ewan in particular was acutely aware of the desire to rush on all the time. It annoyed me too, but I was conscious of the huge miles and the fact that we had to make the ferry in Aswan next Saturday, or we'd lose a week. We couldn't afford that because we'd made a commitment to UNICEF in Ethiopia.

Ewan and I are very different personalities; it's the same with Russ and David and when the four of us are involved in something as complicated and hazardous as this it can become a little tense.

Four strong-minded and very forthright people: Russ is a problem solver, he sees the situation and sets about finding whatever resolution is required, like pressing on and making the time we needed. I'm like that, seeking the destination; I suppose it's the racer in me.

Ewan, on the other hand, is a thinker with a different mindset completely, as is David. Already that dynamic was becoming apparent and bringing with it the attendant tensions.

EWAN: I didn't come here just to get to Cape Town, I came to experience Africa on a motorbike. The deadline was the ferry, however, at the bottom of Egypt, and we were committed to making it. But I was worried about just pressing on and on and not seeing anything.

Our second day in Tunisia, we headed for Matmata. This was where George Lucas filmed the first *Star Wars* movie, specifically Luke Skywalker's house carved into the rock.

We parked and the air was livid with heat. We sat for a moment just gazing across an amazing desert vista of low hills and stunted bushes. Since the last town the road had been climbing, with the hills growing up in layers of sandstone like great piles of pancakes abutting the side of the road.

We met this lad who spoke English while we were having coffee and he offered to be our guide. Lots of people had offered but he was mellow and laid-back. He took us to the caves, first pointing out a couple of flat rock slabs with metal hatches set into the

One of the troglodyte houses at Matmata.

surface. Opening one we realised it was a well. We could smell the water, see our reflections fifteen feet below. He explained that there were more than a hundred troglodyte houses dug into the soft sandstone; people had lived here for seven hundred years and they still collected their water.

We gazed down on an amazing courtyard with arched portals cut into the rock; it must have been twenty or so feet below ground level and climbing down we found an old woman who invited us into her home.

Inside it was light, airy and surprisingly spacious; flat bronze plates hung on the walls as ornaments and she sat us down in alcoves laid with ornamental blankets. She boiled tea in a large kettle, pouring it from a great height and finally stirred in spoonfuls of sugar. She told us that in summer the heat in town got to some fifty degrees and it was much cooler here.

' Once you got away from the city the quality of tarmac declined considerably, with potholes and sand encroaching from either side. The whole place had a parched feel, the air hot and dry. ' CHARLEY

2

LIBYA

HERE'S SAND IN YOUR EYE!

EWAN: Six hours later we were beyond the border and riding into a sand storm. The air was burning my throat and we seemed to have the world and his wife escorting us: whatever we wanted to do in Libya, we'd not be doing it alone.

Leaving Tunisia had been complicated by the fact that David and Jimmy weren't allowed into Libya despite everyone in the office and our travel advisers Explore trying their best to get them in. It was a disappointment but not unexpected. They were flying to Geneva then Cairo and inadvertently they left us with a vehicle problem. David had the Tunisian authority for one Nissan stamped into his passport and therefore we'd nothing to certify that the truck had ever been allowed in. There was a mini drama, but between them Russ and Jim managed to smooth things over.

In the end we were through and immediately everything altered. All we'd done was travel a little further down the same stretch of tarmac but the landscape looked different; it *felt* different. The wind had picked up and it brought the sand, hot stinging grains; it was like driving into a blast heater.

The people were friendly but the driving went rapidly downhill – most of the cars we encountered seemed to stick to the back wheel, nosing us along.

This country was poorer, a dictatorship, an Islamic state with borders that had been closed to westerners for many years. There was a distinct military feel. We were in convoy, heading for Tripoli and we had no choice but to follow Nuri, our fixer.

The land was flat. Electricity pylons dominated the skyline. The trees were short and looked half-grown and sand filled the air.

We followed the cars to some ruins – the ancient town of Sabrata. For a while it wasn't clear whether we would be allowed to film – the guides seemed to want us there to help promote tourism, but at the same time they told us that filming was forbidden. Used to being yoked to an absolute system they now seemed weighed down by indecision.

In the end we passed inside. It was worth the toing and froing with the guides – it really was magnificent; another massive Roman amphitheatre with huge pillars and what looked like Botticelli cupids scrolled into the stonework.

We climbed the steps into roofless, doorless rooms that were cut in sandstone. We came to a small courtyard and Charley suggested it might have been for concession stands or where they sold beer maybe: immediately I went into bartender mode.

CHARLEY: Ewan wanted to know if Romans had beer and I had no idea. He was serving though and I leant on the imaginary bar.

'What'll it be, sir?' he asked me. 'What can I get you?'

'A flagon of wine and, er, a glass of sherry for the wife.'

'Right, sir, coming up.' He was pouring from an imaginary pump. 'Come to see the lions, have you, sir?'

'Naw, here to see that famous Charley Boorman gladiator.'

Left: A classic pose from the Long Way Round days . . .

'You know,' Ewan said, 'he's not bad, but he's not all he's cracked up to be.'

'He's the only reason I came,' I said sourly. 'Got any crisps? Actually forget the crisps; I'll take a bag of pig's ears instead.'

'Got some in the back, sir,' Ewan sought pig's ears. 'Yeah, he's all right that Boorman, but he's not all he's cracked up to be.' He handed me the bag. 'That'll be fifteen Roman shekels.'

CHARLEY: We climbed to the top tier of stone seats and got a fantastic view to the shore and the remains of the rest of the buildings. But it was getting late and our guides had booked hotels for us in the capital.

A few miles with crazy drivers, absolute nutters, and we passed under a massive metal arch and were really in Gaddafi country now; his picture was everywhere: on billboards, buildings, in the hotel lobby.

By now I was knackered. In my room I put my boots on the balcony and squeezed the damp from my pillow. We'd see David and Jimmy again in Egypt but we had a long way to go before that. My mind began to race through how little time we had, how many miles we had to do . . .

EWAN: I was equally worried about making the ferry that would take us the length of Lake Nasser and the thought of racing on and on all the time was beginning to piss me off. We had only six days and there was every chance we'd be held up at the Egyptian border. Even if we weren't, we still had to get all the way down the Nile. Fuck, the last thing I'd wanted to be was a slave to the clock.

CHARLEY: Riding through Libya following a van full of official people makes it very difficult to meet anyone, and perhaps that influenced our decision as much as the time pressure we were under. We'd left Tripoli at eight o'clock and it was already thirty-three degrees. Ewan pulled alongside me. 'Hey, Charley, only thirty-three. Christ it's fucking freezing.'

Tripoli's a pleasant, atmospheric city, and we rode through the centre, coming to Green Square where an old fort overlooked a lake. The buildings were two storeys, white mostly, and seemed all but untouched by tourism – and there were minibuses crammed with people everywhere.

Out of the city we could see warships at anchor just offshore. And everywhere I looked there were thousands of plastic bags, plastic containers, just dumped. After the cleanliness of Tunisia it gave the whole place a down-at-heel, ugly feel.

Once you got away from the city the quality of tarmac declined considerably, with potholes and sand encroaching from either side. The whole place had a parched feel, the air hot and dry. Apparently there are no natural rivers in Libya only wadis: valleys that hold water after periods of heavy rain. The lack of natural flowing water was

The incredible ancient
city of Leptis Magna.

evident in the atmosphere; there was not even a vague sense of freshness even though it
was early morning.

EWAN: The litter was oppressive and with it that insistent odour of garbage. But I was
excited about the ancient city we were heading for. Our guide was called Iystiri and for
eight years he'd been showing people the magnificence of Leptis Magna.

It had been established about 1100 BC, but it's mainly known as the city of Septimius
Severus. A native of Leptis Magna, he became Emperor of Rome in the second century
and died in York, of all places. Just as we'd ridden the Appian Way, Charley and I now
walked a road that led from the great arch of Septimius all the way to Alexandria: in the
other direction it had stretched to Carthage.

The arch was incredible – it had been reconstructed in 1920 by a group of Italian
archaeologists who had excavated the stones. The road was exquisitely paved and
stretched as far as the eye could see about six feet below the level of the sand. Some of
the stones were decorated with images of Septimius and his sons.

There were also huge triangles and our guide explained that they were in fact
Venetian, from a much later period, put there to keep evil spirits away.

There were eight Corinthian pillars with eight Gods, palm in one hand and crown in the other, and four spread eagles, the ancient symbol of power. We could see ramparts, remnants of the old walls that in the city's heyday had run for three kilometres. We saw images of the Gods: Diana in her short skirt and Apollo naked.

'Well hung,' Charley commented quietly. 'Well, he is a God after all.'

Some of what we were exploring had been discovered as late as 1962 and the excavation was still going on three years ago. Charley was shaking his head in wonder. 'Imagine finding it,' he said. 'Digging it up and realising what you had: it must have been incredible. There used to be shops right here. And houses, business places and people.'

'Not so many mopeds though,' I put in.

'No, right: I bet they had those little chariots to tear about in, the kids I mean, you know, drawn by greyhounds or something.'

CHARLEY: We came to a corner where our guide pointed out another cosmic battle; this time the defender of the city was a winged penis. Yes, that's right, a winged penis doing battle with the evil eye.

According to Iystiri the penis fought the eye to keep evil spirits away. The piece of limestone where the battle was captured had been there since the second century so we just *had* to press a palm against it for luck. Ewan looked sideways at me. 'Well, mate. We've touched a penis in Libya. Not what we set out to do perhaps, but a winged penis at least.'

We came to an open, grassy area, a kind of sports field, and across the street were the remains of the public baths.

The wind had picked up and was bringing sand, very hot and hard on the eyes – a warning of what was to come. The guide led us through the baths, showing us the outside pool first, the floor of which had been mosaic, the sides marble. He took us to what he called a 'hot room', showed us where the pipes came in – one for hot water and one for cold; the hot water heated by massive furnaces.

Above each furnace was a cistern holding water and slaves worked all the time to keep the fires burning. Hot air was captured and pumped through tiles in a flue system that was covered over with marble. Heated walls and floor – the engineering was incredible and this all went back to the second century. They even had a sewerage system complete with communal toilets.

Iystiri took us into the forum or marketplace that had pillars running the perimeter in a rectangle. There had been a portico built above them housing lots of stalls, shops and arcades; the central area had been open to the air. One wall was intact and it gave us a tremendous sense of how it would have been: the hustle and bustle of trading – cloths, fruit, spices, incense maybe, even livestock and slaves. The entrances had been decorated with the heads of two gods, one of which was Medusa with the snakes in her hair.

Ewan and Charley
discuss the finer points
of Roman hygiene.

From the forum we went to the Severan Basilica, originally the law courts but, after the Romans converted to Christianity, this place had become a church decorated by stones carved with griffins.

EWAN: The basilica really made an impression on me. I loved the griffins, who had the body of a lion with the head and wings of an eagle. Iystiri told us they symbolised eternity. I found it moving, the thought of this ancient civilisation, long gone, painting images of things they believed would last for ever.

The whole place was amazing, so unexpected and moving, and as near a glimpse of everyday Roman life as you could get. I had such a vivid image of the people of Leptis Magna going about their lives. I was reminded again of how important it was to stop and take time out from the journey.

Back at the bikes, we had a major discussion with Russ about what we were going to do next. The choice was either to stick to the coast road and see places like Benghazi and probably not make the Aswan ferry, or speed across the desert road tomorrow. The ferry took us to Sudan and it only went once a week. If we missed it, we would be turning our schedule upside down.

Charley was mulling it over: 'I know we're rushing, but what choice do we have?'

'We have to think about the UNICEF visits,' I put in. 'Of course we should try to make the ferry. But if we're on the motorcycles all the time, I'm afraid we'll miss things.'

Russ shook his head. 'We just have to find the right balance between doing the miles and getting off the bikes.'

Charley cut in again. 'We're going to have that issue of how much time we spend in each place the whole way down, aren't we?'

Russ pointed out that with minders around all the time, it was much harder to break free and meet people in Libya. He was also aware that simply riding 420 miles through the desert in the scorching heat would be a challenge in itself. 'Ball-breaking stuff,' he added.

He had a point.

CHARLEY: We left Leptis Magna under dull and overcast skies, yet the heat was still ridiculous. Already the wind was beginning to pick up; it had been whistling through the ruins and that was ominous.

Still I was thinking of what lay ahead. Stupid ferry and only six days to get there. The thing was that if we missed it, then our trip to see Riders for Health, plus three UNICEF visits, would turn into a nightmare. It was crazy, but then again it was crazy following a white van all day and stopping every couple of miles at army checkpoints. And I have to admit the thought of rattling through the desert was pretty cool.

The driving seemed even more erratic now it was getting dark. There were lorries all over the place, so we had to take great care overtaking. Every time we did we were buffeted hard by the wind.

The camp site was half a dozen flat-roofed buildings hugging a dirty beach. Ewan and I took a long look at the sea then we parked up and I grabbed my tent. The wind was howling, really loud, whipping my hair across my face and this didn't bode well.

EWAN: All night the wind gusted and the tent would billow to the point of the poles almost breaking. I lay there with my feet pressed to the sides and my arms spread, using my weight to stop the tent blowing away.

The sides rattled, a terrible racket as if someone was shaking stones in a can. It got louder and louder and, grabbing my head torch, I saw the bell end whipping wildly. Sand had crept into the tent and coated everything.

Outside I checked the pole footings and re-fixed elastic guys, burying the pegs while the hot wind dragged my hair so hard it hurt.

I must have slept because I woke up. The first sound I heard was the wind, my first thought was that we had 420 miles to cover today. I was itchy and bleary. Everything was coated in sand, everything.

We got going by eight, heading for Tobruk. And what a day it turned out to be: hour after hour, the land bleak to the point of depressing. Police checkpoints, military, always following the white van driven by Nuri and the man from the secret service. I was filthy, my stuff was filthy, sand everywhere.

Mercifully it was cooler. Yesterday it had been thirty-three degrees, this morning it was a pleasant twenty-four. We rolled on and on, nothing but telegraph poles, desert and the perpetual wind that bent the bike to weird angles, willing it to tip over; a wind that forced my head to the side so I had to strain every muscle to keep upright.

For the first time I passed a sign written in English: *Africa constitutes one nation of a thousand tribes*. I'd try to remember that.

Camels wandered loose off to my left and I imagined what it would be like if one lumbered across the road in the swirl of nothingness created by this storm. Terrifying. As if to accentuate the point I saw something up ahead and slowed to a stop. Charley came alongside and we inspected the carcass of one such beast shredded by the side of the road. Its flesh had been picked clean; the skull exposed. We could see smashed ribs and, where its stomach had been, a pile of half digested grass.

We rode on and the road kill got worse: camels, a cow, dogs, sheep . . . you name it, it had been killed on this road. That was the theme of the day: flying sand and road kill.

But despite all this, it was exhilarating, too. We passed an oil field, flames snaking skyward from a massive chimney. It was bitter, stark. We stopped at yet another checkpoint and as we pulled away, as if in defiance, Charley hoiked the front wheel.

SANDSTORM

The sand wrapped around us, cutting the bikes off from each other so I could barely make out my mate's tail lights. With every gust of wind the bike would try to crash: wind would catch in the panniers, weigh against the massive fuel tank, swirling about the bars it would try to tip me off.

Incredible, this desolate fantastic place that was Libya.

CHARLEY: We passed a car lumbering along on the wrong side of the road, the driver with no idea what the fuck he was doing. We passed lorries with no lights that just appeared from the sand fog to create wind blast that shook the bikes. It was almost four and we hadn't eaten since breakfast. All I could see was sand, dust and fucking plastic. The stench of rubbish carried on the wind. The fun of it, the challenge was dissipating and I was fed up with being battered. I was sick of sand getting under my visor and into my eyes, of cramping hands where I was gripping so hard my injuries from the Dakar plagued me. I'd had a gutful of the smell of garbage and dead animals.

It grew steadily darker: the sun just a hazy reddened ball. Most of the time I couldn't see a fucking thing and this was getting dangerous. Yet I was picking up speed, blatting through with bugger-all visibility at more than seventy. I suppose, when I think about it, it was some kind of fun. I thought, yeah, and whatever happens, happens.

By seven o'clock it was almost dark and the world just seemed to shut down. Fuck a duck, this was crazy. The weather had closed in so badly now our speed had dropped to fifteen mph. What were we doing, riding this road in a sandstorm and possibly into the night?

I passed a pile of broken toilets right by the side of the road. I couldn't believe it: a great load of smashed porcelain that some trucker had just tipped out. I almost didn't see it and you crash into that and you're toast.

By 8.15 it was pitch black, the wind still blowing – but no sand. It was clear and for the first time that day luck seemed to be with us.

It didn't last long.

Dai noticed black smoke kicking out of Russ's Nissan. They started losing power and we all pulled over. Within minutes Jim had his head torch on and was crawling over the engine. The air filter was clogged with sand – he knocked it clean against the running board. They had been using snorkels to ram air through the turbo but instead they were actually sucking the sand in. Ewan twisted the snorkel round so the intake faced back instead of forward.

We got going again. But they were still losing power and had to pull over a second time. Now 'Mr Fix-it' was working on the connections for the turbo.

We'd been on this road for thirteen hours and after another thirty minutes we got moving a second time, though Russ and Jim could only pootle at forty-five. I heard that Russ had been on the phone to an RAC man back in London and he'd given them a few tips. He wasn't planning a roadside recovery, mind you.

EWAN: Nuri, our fixer, was trying to get a mechanic organised for when – and if – we finally got to Tobruk. I couldn't believe the weather, so much sand. It was in every orifice in my body. Charley was alongside me. 'Did you hear Russ spoke to the RAC?' he called across the radio.

I nodded. It was weird to think of some RAC man back in England getting a call from Russ in a sandstorm in the Libyan desert.

'He's amazing in situations like this,' Charley added. 'He stays incredibly calm and never gives up.'

I felt sick with muscle ache but ahead of us at last were the lights of Tobruk. With the end in sight I brightened. We had ridden the desert trail in a monster sandstorm and still reached our destination. It felt like a huge achievement – really exhilarating.

It was after eleven when we finally got off the bikes. I dragged my helmet over my head, my eyes running from wind and sand.

'Deserve a little shower,' Charley said. 'Don't we?'

Nuri came over and told us he'd found a mechanic. 'I tell you,' he said, 'I've never seen sand storming for twenty-four hours. The miles we covered in those conditions, it's amazing.' He smiled then and taking our passports turned to go inside. 'Yeah,' he added. 'The Force is strong with you guys.'

8

ICE COLD IN ALEX

CHARLEY: I woke up feeling worse than when I went to sleep. I suppose I did feel some sense of satisfaction, but it was tempered by the danger we'd put ourselves in. I wasn't sure if it had been worth it.

I had quite a view, mind you – the contrasts of Libya. In the distance the massive Tobruk power plant, in the foreground a terrace and the crystal blue of the sea.

And the Nissan was fixed. Last night before I went to bed I saw Jim under the bonnet again and he told me a pipe had slipped off the turbo. With that in place everything should be working as normal.

God, what a journey.

EWAN: Both Charley and I were emotional enough already after yesterday's epic ride. We hadn't prepared ourselves for how the war graves at Tobruk would affect us.

The cemetery was in the middle of nowhere, a massive place with beautiful sandstone walls and a pitched roof portico at the entrance. It was a tranquil place tended by an elderly Libyan man who acted as our guide. Through the gate we were greeted by a path of baked earth that led to the first of three memorials. There was one for Australians, another for Poles and a third for Czech fighters.

Our guide told us that British soldiers lay here as well as New Zealand, South African and Yugoslavian forces. And lying next to them, with their headstones facing Mecca, were Muslim dead from Libya, Algeria, Sudan and India.

The place was beautifully kept, with cactus growing in spiky flowers between the silent graves. We came across many plots whose occupants were unknown, the same inscription on all of them: 'Soldier of the 1939–45 war, known to God'.

CHARLEY: I walked among the stones, trying to imagine the men who lay there, who they'd been and how they'd died, how their families had learned of the tragedy.

Back on the bikes all I could think about were those young men who'd died – and about Telsche, my sister. I missed her so much it hurt. She'd been so young, so beautiful and riding along I cried my eyes out, blubbering away in my helmet on the flat, dusty road to the Egyptian border.

In a café in Egypt, watching a news report on the unfolding tragedy in Darfur.

EWAN: We stopped for lunch not far from the Libyan–Egyptian border and found the BBC news playing on the TV in the corner. The report was about the horrors in Darfur; the Bush administration using the term genocide to describe what was happening.

The fighting has been raging in the western part of the country since 2003. On one side there's a militia called Janjaweed, mostly nomads from the north. On the other is the Sudanese Liberation Movement, mostly farmers. Whilst publicly denying it, the Sudanese government has funded the northern militia and joined in with attacks on the tribes from which the Liberation Movement is drawn.

It was a complex situation, but when the populations of entire villages were raped and killed, the bodies thrown down the drinking wells, it ceased to be complex and just came down to right and wrong.

CHARLEY: It took five hours to cross into Egypt. Not too bad really and I pulled the obligatory wheelie.

Although the landscape looked much the same, we had crossed to another country and the difference was as discernible as when we passed from Tunisia into Libya. Here in Egypt, everything already looked fresher, cleaner . . . wealthier.

We watched some women about to cross from Egypt into Libya, hoisting their skirts up then taping up the knees of the massive bloomers they were wearing. It was the oddest thing I've seen at a border crossing. Once the tape was in place they stuffed box after box of cigarettes down their pants in full view of us, the guards, everyone. They'd cross into Libya and sell them for ten dollars a carton then come back for some more – capitalism at work.

Egypt was clearly busier; the towns we went through were bustling with shops and markets, open-air stalls packed with produce. The cars were better quality too, though not a lot safer. The road started climbing and we hit some bends, a welcome distraction from the arrow-straight tarmac of yesterday.

EWAN: We met up with David and Jimmy and it was great to have the whole team together again. We were off again, in convoy. Alexandria was 506 kilometres away and we'd be there for lunch tomorrow.

The climb into the twisty stuff was invigorating, a beautiful bay in the distance and once again the kind of bends where you really don't want to make a mistake. It was now getting dark, we were an hour beyond the border and Charley and I rode two abreast.

In the thick of it: traffic in Alexandria.

We passed through towns, no pavements, just sand stretching to apartment buildings and market stalls, and men in robes would wave and nod – and beyond the town into the desert, a full moon hovered above the highway. It was beautiful and I thought, God I'm riding through Egypt. The sky was purple and blue, no light pollution, and as darkness took hold the blend of colours was amazing.

We rode into the night, something we'd vowed we wouldn't do. The best laid plans, eh? Lights flickered on the horizon now, the town of Marsa Matruh.

The following day we were in three lanes of motorway and the massive sprawl of Alexandria loomed on our left. To our right there was the stillness of a bay where the water looked almost pink. The traffic was manic and Charley and I now spent all our time warning each other about the next nutter approaching.

9

PYRAMIDS & PORN

EWAN: Lunch in Alexandria – but we left after we'd eaten. Given the Riders for Health situation it was the best course of action. We hit serious tarmac and really put the hammer down; four lanes of high speed traffic.

For a while it seemed the land was greener, but before we knew it there was the sand again, piles of rock littered the horizon.

Giza – all at once the cars came thick and fast and we were on the outskirts of the town. Cars were hooting, kids yelling from donkey carts and bicycles.

And then there they were. They seemed to grow up from the middle of the town itself. It took a moment to dawn: the pyramids. My God, I'd ridden my motorbike all the way to the great pyramids of Egypt.

Excitement gripped me. We funnelled into traffic; the buildings stained a dirty yellow; apartments, stalls; people everywhere peering at us and waving. We came to a checkpoint and stopped. It was early evening, the sun just beginning to set.

'Hey, Ewan,' Charley said, 'there's a golf course over there. Imagine having a round of golf with the pyramids as your backdrop.' I could hear the enthusiasm in his voice. There's nothing like witnessing one of the great wonders of the world.

Moments later we were moving up to a chequered barrier and the pyramids were right ahead of us. The road was wide and dusty; it snaked a few hundred yards to where the massive stone structures dominated the skyline. As I passed his truck, Ramy, our Egyptian fixer, was standing there in his Indiana Jones hat.

'All yours,' he called.

Initially I didn't understand what he meant. Then I realised – the area was closed off for the evening, and we were the only visitors. I couldn't believe it. We had the pyramids to ourselves. Two colossal structures, they lifted from the desert with Cairo on one side and an ancient expanse of nothingness on the other. I was speechless.

As I rode further, the third one came into view. It was breathtaking. And as Charley pulled up I just thought how inordinately lucky we were. I looked down at the tiny video screen on my bike which tells me what I'm filming and there was Charley Boorman and behind him a fucking pyramid.

CHARLEY: I couldn't get my head round the fact that we were actually here. With the pyramids ahead, I pulled a monumental wheelie.

'Can you believe it, Ewan?' I called. 'It's just incredible.'

The desert was huge and empty, the sun sinking, the sky hazy; it was a fantastic time of day to be there and I knew I'd have to come back soon with Olly and the kids. We could see the lights of Cairo, a massive sprawl and such a contrast with what stood before us.

We moved into the desert so we could see this wonder from a vantage point where there was no road or city. The light was fading quickly now and the desert had an eerie chill to it. The pyramids were shadowy and the sun seemed to bury itself, throwing up a dusty glow like a sandstorm across the horizon. It was an experience I'll never forget, standing with Ewan at the great pyramids of ancient Egypt, five camels being led nose to tail not a hundred yards in front of us.

It was fully dark when Ramy took us inside the pyramid.

No one was allowed in at night and yet here we were. We climbed to the entrance and stepped into a dimly lit tunnel. Floor lamps cast shadows across the stone and Ramy took us up ladders into the grand gallery. He told us there were three burial chambers. One was actually underground and carved into the bedrock; the second was referred to as the Queen's chamber but it had actually contained a statue of the pharaoh Khufu himself. His burial chamber was in the very centre of the pyramid.

Ramy told us the pyramid took about thirty-five years to build and were constructed not by slaves but by a group of very skilled men who worked directly for the king and lived together in construction villages.

EWAN: The kings of Egypt cared more about the afterlife than they did this one: the pyramid would be their house for eternity and it was their life's work to build it. They used two different types of limestone; one for the main blocks and another finer stone for the topmost decorative skin. Ramy explained that much of that stone was missing from this pyramid but you could see it in buildings around Cairo. Over the centuries, people had just viewed the pyramids as old buildings and reclaimed the stone for new construction.

Before we left I stood before the great Sphinx, carved from bedrock in front of the second pyramid, Khafre's. It was like greeting an old friend I'd never met and yet known all my life. I had to pinch myself so I'd know that I really was there, standing in front of it all at last.

CHARLEY: We left the city and hit the bigger roads. We were following the Nile now – riding beside the longest river in the world – with the city on our left and the gloriously lush delta to my right, palm trees and green meadows and beyond them sloping hills.

The Gulf of Suez was behind us, the Red Sea on our left where hundreds of massive ships lay at anchor. Across the Gulf was the Sinai Desert, Israel and Jordan.

We followed the river south and the world opened up again with scrub and sand and a horizon marked with electricity pylons. We passed wind farms and the desert grew rockier. I couldn't believe how much building was going on: blocks of apartments going up all over the desert.

We hit a dual carriageway where the opposing lanes were located a hundred yards across the open scrub. I was rattling along at 80 mph when a car came beetling towards me in what was our outside lane. I had to pull across sharply to avoid hitting it head on. I waved and shouted but the driver just waved back, grinning away as if everything was normal. Which for driving in this country, I suppose it was.

EWAN: We stopped at the Red Sea and Charley and I crossed the road to what looked like a private beach. There was a reed and palm lean-to and a grassy sun canopy. Charley whipped off his clothes and raced down the beach, Jimmy catching his 'ass' on camera. I stripped off and followed him, the water cool and relaxing. It was great – just what we needed after the perils of the road.

Back in the lay-by with the crew we found David and Ramy in fits of laughter. This was indeed a private beach – a military beach. Seeing the bikes, a couple of soldiers had come down to investigate and when they saw cameras and two guys frolicking in the surf naked, they thought we were making gay porn movies. It took a while for Ramy to explain but they were eventually placated.

Can you imagine the headlines? A whole new career for me and Charley . . .

CHARLEY: The checkpoints pissed me off, there were hundreds of them all the way to Luxor. We'd also picked up a police escort, as all tourists have to in this part of Egypt. We stopped to eat at 8.30 and didn't hit Luxor until after midnight. I was shagged out.

But in the morning I woke to a fantastic view of the Nile and beyond it the slopes of pinkish rock that marked the Valley of the Kings.

EWAN: Another extraordinary experience – the Valley of the Kings. For five hundred years the rulers of Egypt's New Kingdom constructed their tombs there, west of the Nile in the Theban Hills.

We crossed the Nile in a small boat with the hills and dunes lifting before us, and that in itself was amazing. We walked pathways between the hills, grey in shadow and pink in the sun; the burial chambers cut deep into the rock.

Ramy took us to the tomb of Seti II. As a man, the Egyptian pharaoh was thought to be the embodiment of Horus, God of the heavens and protector of the Sun God. When he died he became Osiris, King of the Dead and the next pharaoh took on the mantle of Horus.

Seti II only reigned for four years between 1203 and 1197 BC, and his tomb demonstrated as much; the square corridor to the burial chamber was only partially plastered and decorated and the chamber itself just hewn from the rock. There had been no time to complete the tomb because as soon as the king died his path to the afterlife began and he had to be mummified right away. Ramy told us that the bodies were never cut; the organs were removed through the dead man's nose.

'Not his bottom?' I whispered.

'No, his nose.'

Charley gestured. 'I'd have thought . . . you know . . . if there's a hole, use it.'

Ramy explained that the first part of the king's journey would be to stand before the judges, the Gods. Judgement was simple. The king's heart was placed on a set of scales, with a feather on the other. If the heart was heavier than the feather then the king would go to hell. But if he had been a good king and the cares of his heart were few it would be lighter than the feather and he would go to heaven.

> ❛ Here in Kenya, sixteen community health workers were trained to ride the most inhospitable roads in the world. Without them, literally, thousands of people would die. ❜ CHARLEY

10

KENYA

RIDING BIKES & SAVING LIVES

CHARLEY: We managed to get to Aswan while it was still daylight. Even so, I was yawning into my helmet. The city is perched at the top of Lake Nasser and it's from Nasser that we would cross to Sudan. I was a little apprehensive – another country and another set of circumstances; that and the fact that I'd lost my bike document.

All I wanted to do was take a shower, eat and crash. But I had to file a report with the police, which I could then give to customs. I went up to my room, dumped my gear on the bed and splashed cold water over my face. Ewan came in, looking relaxed and with that old sparkle in his eyes.

'You OK, Charley?'

'Fine, mate. What about you?'

'I'm good.' He smiled. 'Have you seen your view?'

'No, I've not had a chance.'

'Take a look at your view, Charley.'

Pulling back the curtains I opened the window and was greeted by one of the most beautiful sights I've ever seen. The dark waters of the lake sparkled in the sunshine; the hotel was perched on a rocky outcrop overlooking single-sail boats with canvas canopies. On the other side a dozen or so more boats were in the shelter of an inlet lined with palm trees. Beyond them I could see another massive ruin, pillars and sandy steps leading down to the water. I could make out ancient roads and walkways, and dominating the whole thing a mass of rolling sand dunes.

Ewan started singing: 'Ruins to the left of me, ruins to the right, here I am, stuck in the middle with me!'

We fell about.

'You know what,' he said, 'this is the trip of a lifetime.'

Slipping my arm around his shoulders we hung out of the window, just gazing across the beauty of the lake.

EWAN: Saturday, and we piled into a minibus for the airport. We were headed for Kenya and Riders for Health, leaving Jim and Dai to get the cars and the bikes to the ferry.

I knew about the charity through the film director Mark Neale, who made the Moto GP documentaries I narrated. This was Charley's deal really, though; he'd been introduced to the organisation by racer Randy Mamola and was more involved than me. I was very interested in their work, however, and couldn't wait to get down there.

Only customs wouldn't let us fly out because according to our passports we had two Nissan trucks and three BMW motorbikes registered to us.

We explained that we were coming back tomorrow but it wasn't enough. Customs needed to physically set eyes on the vehicles before they'd let us board the plane to Kenya. We returned to the hotel, collected the vehicles and drove them back to the customs compound.

We were met, at a very lush and green-looking Nairobi airport, by Andrea and Barry from Riders for Health; they guided us to a small plane that would take us to Mount Kilimanjaro, where motorcycles were taking life-saving resources to remote places. Barry told us that this was a groundbreaker in Kenya, a model for how the idea could work elsewhere.

The plane landed on a red clay airstrip in the middle of the Masai Mara: lion country. We drove across green savannah to the Mbirikani Group Ranch Clinic, a fenced compound where the seriously ill were treated. A series of water towers dominated the gates and open sheds protected a line of 200 cc dirt bikes. They bore the Riders for Health emblem.

We were met by Dr Mariti, tall and smiling and one of four doctors who worked full-time at the clinic.

The idea for some kind of bike outreach had started back in 1988 when Barry and Andrea, together with Randy Mamola, raised money for Save the Children. Invited to a project in Somalia, they discovered a pile of disused motorcycles that they were told were out of commission and saw that with a little care the bikes could easily be put to good use; it was from there the idea of remote access transportation was born.

The incredible workers for Riders for Health

CHARLEY: The idea was to use motorcycles as a method of transporting healthcare to people who'd otherwise die. The principal killer was AIDS but they also dealt with more easily remedied illnesses like dysentery and malaria.

The advent of antiretroviral drugs and the fact that they were finally being manufactured in Africa meant that in principle more people could be treated. Not if they had to walk seventy kilometres to get the treatment, though, or, in the case of HIV, three hundred. Before Riders for Health got involved in this area, the nearest HIV treatment had been Nairobi, and most people were either too poor or too sick to get there.

Here in Kenya sixteen community health workers were trained to ride the most inhospitable roads in the world. Without them, literally thousands of people would die. Their basic supplies are simple: mosquito bed nets, blood-testing equipment, the required drugs and a 70/30 corn and soya food supplement – it's pointless administering life-saving medicine if the patient still suffers from malnutrition.

The health workers are backed by fifteen nurses and four doctors, as well as four full-time lab assistants. Mbirikani is totally self-contained, the compound made up of a number of Nissen huts, the whole place enclosed by a wire fence. We wandered over to the bikes and the workshop where they were maintained. This really cool guy in a white shirt and thick black braces was in charge and Ewan and I were in our element.

These bikes had been modified with twin side stands and crash bars on the engine casing and handlebars, as well as reinforced metal racks to carry the top boxes. The workshop carried every spare imaginable and all the riders were trained in basic maintenance.

Mounting up, we followed our guide out of the compound and a few miles up the dirt road to a small cluster of huts dwarfed by Mount Kilimanjaro. The huts had thatched roofs and the walls were made from mud or animal excrement. We were there to see Agnes, a woman in her thirties, hair plaited and wearing a sand-coloured dress with a brightly coloured bracelet on her wrist. She was surrounded by half a dozen smiling women, all dressed in vivid colours with a mass of laughing children at their feet.

Agnes was the first person to have been treated by the clinic at Mbirikani; infected with the HIV virus, she was bedridden and helpless. She weighed forty-six kilos when they found her and, like thousands of others in Africa, she had effectively been left to die. Now she weighed sixty-four kilos and looked terrific. She was happy to stand there with cameras and chat about what had happened to her. I thought she might have carried some stigma with the other villagers but in fact the reverse was true. Most people had known her when she was dying and here she was, proof that the medical facility was working – and the inspiration for other people to come forward and be tested for HIV.

She remains on antiretroviral drugs, of course, which are brought to her by a community health worker on a motorcycle. That means she doesn't miss her dosage, which is absolutely critical.

Our guide was one of the community health workers who'd grown up in this village and he told us the unit dealt with five hundred outpatients, all of whom were visited on motorbikes. They don't just treat HIV or tuberculosis – they also bring simple sanitation equipment that means the difference between life and death, like the plastic portaloo we could see under the shadow of the mountain. Ewan commented that this had to be the world's most scenic toilet. 'Imagine that view,' he said, 'Kilimanjaro in snowy splendour after your morning doings.'

EWAN: Agnes was an amazing woman and living proof that the project was successful. HIV was one thing – I've been involved in Malawi and seen the devastation it can cause – but what amazed me most was the simplest of things. The project covers a seventy kilometre radius and when it started they'd encounter two to three hundred cases of malaria each year. The introduction of bed nets had reduced that rate to almost zero. Incredible to think that a net costing no more than a couple of quid saves so many lives each year.

It wasn't just a case of handing them out, mind you; it was bringing the washing solution to make sure they were re-treated, it was showing people how to tuck them in so the bed was secure, it was follow-up visits to make sure the nets were working. The health workers didn't just call on the patients either; prevention being better than cure, they visited schools to educate children; they spoke to mothers, young women, village elders.

They had a total of 2500 patients in the HIV programme. On discharge from the clinic all patients became the subject of visits from the community health workers, who made sure they took their medication, kept up with sanitation and, where necessary, received food supplements.

I spoke to Dr Mariti about pregnant women and the way HIV is often passed from mother to baby through the mother's milk. In Malawi women were treated with antiretroviral drugs early in pregnancy but were told to breastfeed their babies because the water was so bad formula feeding would be impossible.

Here the Prevention of Mother to Child Transmission Protocol was completely different; they advocated that formula milk should be used. The health workers carried water-purifying sachets and as long as these were used when mixing the baby formula there was no risk of waterborne disease.

The doctor told me that since the clinic opened they had successfully delivered 110 babies, who didn't carry the virus, from HIV positive mothers. In fact the only babies they'd 'lost' had already been born when their mothers came in.

CHARLEY: My mate in the white shirt and braces was showing me the bikes in detail: 200 cc was the right size machine for the terrain and what they were carrying, light enough to be manoeuvrable yet with enough power to cope with the dodgy roads.

Every morning before setting off for the day the riders do what my man called PLANS, which was a basic bike check: Petrol, Lubrication, Adjustments, Nuts and bolts. The S was for Stop, i.e. the brakes and tyres.

They had fuel facilities on site and made sure they had enough in the bikes for that day; they oiled and greased working parts; they checked engine and gearbox oil. They tested front and rear brakes and meticulously scoured the tyres for cuts and nicks. They carried tyre levers, inner tubes and repair kits and I could only imagine the speed you'd fix that puncture knowing a pride of lions was watching you.

Each morning they'd check the chain for movement – a maximum of 20 mm play was the marker. They checked nuts and bolts because they worked loose almost every day given the harsh country these bikes were ridden through.

The training was taught by Riders for Health, starting with the basics like balance and throttle control, moving on to braking safely, emergency braking, cornering and dealing with the likes of gravel, sand and mud. They taught defensive riding – how to deal with errant minibus drivers, for example. We were told about one young nurse who saw a bus coming for her, shifted the bike off the road and parked. Somehow the bus still hit her, breaking her leg, the poor soul.

It was a brilliant day, really informative and relaxing. The work is invaluable, the most effective answer to the problems of reaching people in remote areas; I could see it working all over the world. The bikes last five or six years because they are prepared properly and well maintained. That in itself was a major achievement because normally a bike would last about six months on these kinds of roads.

I was hugely impressed with the Masai people; tall and elegant, confident and incredibly well spoken. Most of the riders were from the local area. It was a real community thing; they were saving lives, riding bikes and creating jobs. It had been the highlight of the journey so far for me.

The following day we met up with Richard Branson who was in Kenya donating motorcycles. It was because of him that we'd been able to grab a plane in Aswan. We had lunch at an old colonial house with wild boar and a giraffe called Lyn in the garden. We chatted about all things African and the three of us rode around a mini dirt track for photographers.

The end of a fantastic couple of days and Ewan and I were buzzing. One of the great privileges of doing these trips is being able to witness first-hand the achievements of the charities we're involved with. It's humbling to find so many people so keen to make things better; humbling and uplifting; hopeful when you contrast it with the news reports we'd seen from Darfur. For every warmongering, power-hungry psychopath there

Richard Branson is also a supporter of Riders for Health. These few motorbikes will make a huge difference in saving people's lives.

are hundreds of normal people going about their business quietly ensuring the human race retains some dignity.

EWAN: Back on the plane to Aswan and then we had the sand of Sudan to negotiate; but before we got there we had twenty-four hours travelling the length of Lake Nasser and I was really looking forward to that.

BLAZING SADDLES

11

SUDAN

THE STUFF OF DREAMS

EWAN: We were at the docks by 8.30 and I was finally witnessing what I'd hoped to find when we steamed into Tunisia. A medley of vehicles, people, boxes, packing cases, sacks of everything imaginable; one truck so overloaded the wheel arches scraped the tyres and the load itself was the size of another lorry. Everywhere it was bedlam; a mass of buses and cars, pickup trucks, noise and colour – at last I'd found my scene from Indiana Jones.

Charley looked as excited as I felt.

'Fantastic, Charley, isn't it?' I said.

'A boat to Sudan. It's brilliant!'

CHARLEY: The boat was chaotic and yet at the same time strangely organised. Noise everywhere, people shouting and loading so much stuff, fridges shifted end over end and piled on top of everything else and everything piled on top of them.

We'd boarded at 11.30 and now it was 5.30 and still we'd yet to pull away from the wharf. I asked one of the crew when we were leaving and he told me this was African time and to leave that watch behind. He was right. People were still coming aboard, laden with beds and wicker chairs, TV sets and cases of soft drinks. We chatted to people, we shook hands and told them our names, the atmosphere so lively and infectious.

Finally we got going, leant on the rail between the rows of orange lifebelts as the horn blew loud enough to deafen.

EWAN: 'President Nasser flooded this lake,' Charley said.

I gazed across open water to where the horizon drifted. 'Maybe he needed somewhere to swim.'

'I think it was his mausoleum, his pyramid, his everlasting mark on Egyptian history. They say the whole area was covered in artefacts: it was a real kick-bollock and scramble to get it all out.'

We were up by the bridge and the captain was shouting at his crew, five of them standing across the bridge, the guy at the wheel with barely enough room to move. The captain looked like something from a Sinbad movie; old and gnarled, great thick fingers with calluses all over them. He was wearing a long white robe and white cloth wrapped around his head. He had fierce eyes, sharp like a hawk's. He kept glowering our way and every time we approached he'd shout at someone and we'd back off.

'I think he's barking,' I said softly.

We met Dave and Amelia. Dave was from Australia and was backpacking around the continent, Amelia was headed for Darfur and a summer of volunteer work. They'd just hooked up together as travellers often do. We spoke about Aswan and the Temple of Isis and the little sarcophagus that had carried Tutankhamen's organs. Of course that brought us back to hooks and noses and bottoms and I was at pains to point out that your bottom is a larger orifice than your nose.

Later in my cabin I hung out the window. The sun was going down, the sky plum coloured and the water almost black. I watched as it grew darker and darker and then finally the sun seemed to hiss into the lake and for a moment the whole sky blazed gold.

I took a moment to reflect and knew instinctively that there had been something really important about going to Kenya. I thought the riders had the best job in the world, riding bikes to keep people alive.

CHARLEY: Waking early I knocked on Ewan's door. We were passing Abu Simbel and I didn't want him to miss it – though this wasn't the original site. Built in the thirteenth century BC, it was moved in the 1960s just before Nasser flooded the place.

It was a couple of flat-topped bluffs the colour of the desert. The sky was a thin blue, that early morning stillness about it. From a distance the structure looked like a sloping hillside with tall shadowy portals cut into it. When you looked closer, of course, they weren't portals, but massive figures, four of them sculpted from the stone, built by Ramasses II as a monument to himself and his queen.

Afternoon tea,
Sudan style.

EWAN: We'd crossed a line of floating barrels that spanned the lake, the border I assumed, which meant we were now on Lake Nubia in Sudan, close to the port at Wadi Halfa. I could see desert stretching away to the horizon.

We tied off at the grimy, oil-stained docks at 11.30 and at two p.m. we were still on the boat. We'd tried to get off but it was a rugby scrum and officials from Sudan made sure that despite the mass of heaving, sweating humanity it was paramount that a photocopier disembarked first. A couple of cops were barking at everyone.

Finally we did get off and everything was unloaded. It was five kilometres to the customs compound where the barge carrying our vehicles had docked. Along with about a hundred other people we jammed onto the bus. Sweat was pouring off us now, the heat like nothing I'd ever experienced; it had to be well into the forties.

At the customs yard we checked the bikes then settled down for the carnets to be worked through. There were two massive customs sheds and lots of men in blue uniforms but it was almost six by the time we were finished.

CHARLEY: We camped beside one of the few hills dotted across the land. Apart from that it was sun-baked sand in all directions. I'd been told the road was dirt most of the way to Khartoum and that was nearly eight hundred miles. I couldn't wait to get started. First though, I adjusted the suspension on the bikes to make sure we had the play we needed, then reduced the tyre pressures.

I hadn't decided whether to put my tent up or sleep on one of the bivouac bed mats as Ewan was planning. Dai, however, already had a hammock slung between the bull bars of the two Nissans and he was lying back clutching an inflatable sheep.

I burst out laughing. Russ came alongside, shaking his head sadly. 'A Welshman and a sheep,' he said. 'We should have thought about that.'

'Have you met Barbara, Charley?' Dai was in fits. 'I was keeping her till morale got low but ... Anyway, she's ready and ... We're going to snuggle up together later.'

12

SUDAN

THE SAND IN SUDAN

CHARLEY: I woke early, itching to get riding. But no sooner were we on the bikes than Ewan hit deep sand. His front wheel washed out, the bike went down and he was off.

'My least comfortable surface, Charley.' Ewan was up and checking the bike. 'The only sand I remember is the beach in Wales when the police chased us off.'

'Remember what I told you: lean back on the pegs, dump the clutch and use the throttle. Look ahead as far as you can and if you get in trouble throttle your way out. If you come to deeper sand then lean back a little more. Oh, and avoid the tyre tracks. Always go virgin; once you get in the wheel ruts you'll be stuck. Cut across them to get to the smoother stuff.'

I really felt for Ewan. I love off-road riding, it's dangerous and unpredictable but massive fun. I'd trained for a year before I did the Dakar. Ewan doesn't even ride off-road for a hobby. Sand is different from any other surface, really hard to judge and you either love it or hate it. Ewan hates it, but hats off to him because he was in the saddle again and sliding the back end all the way to the hard stuff.

God, it was hot, not much after nine and really beginning to boil. We weren't wearing jackets, just the inners with the armour attached and for the first time we were sporting knee braces. Standing on the pegs is tiring and the braces give support to the joint, stop it hyper-extending when you're bouncing around.

We were headed for Dongola where we would cross the Nile and I was enjoying myself immensely. The scenery was incredible, vast and empty – and beautiful. The road was barely discernible; the only demarcation the slight rise at the edges, otherwise it was the same colour, the same texture almost, as the rest of the scenery – a dusty floor in every direction. Above it a sky so clear it looked as though it was melting.

EWAN: I'd already drunk most of the water in my camel pack. There's a tube attachment and you bite down then suck the liquid up. It was a good job we were carrying plenty in the panniers.

I'm not comfortable in the sand. Charley was great, though; helping me out and passing on the advice that had served him so well. I was doing it now, up on the pegs and leaning back and watching the road instead of my front wheel.

This was fantastic: truly Lawrence of Arabia country. We were climbing, the sand was changing colour, there were more rocks and the road was a real boneshaker. I could feel the bike begin to vibrate and made a point of staying loose and relaxed. I could feel my feet burning – like they were being boiled in a bag. The discomfort however was negated by where we were; it made me tingle just to look around.

Ahead I saw Charley wobble on his arse, his feet were off the pegs. Seconds later I was on the same patch. The bike wagged its head savagely but I held my nerve and kept the throttle open. Yes! I was through, adrenalin pumping, suddenly exhilarated.

Fifty yards further Charley pulled to the side. 'Claudio's down,' he said.

I looked round and saw Claudio's bike on its side and pointing back the way we had come. He was on his feet, though, thank God.

'Typical.' Charley had his helmet off and started walking back. 'He always did like to crash in spectacular style.'

When we got to him Claudio was checking the patch of sand. 'I was too close to you, I didn't see it. Look, it's so fine, it looks like concrete dust, really.'

'Fesh fesh,' Charley said. 'Really deep fine sand. It just sucks you in.'

'Are you all right, Claudio?' I asked him.

'Fine. The bike though, she's looking in the other direction so I don't know what happened.'

Typical Claudio, he just took it in his stride.

Charley checked the bike. The controls were all working, the fluid reservoirs intact. Taking a big rock he set about knocking the really bent pannier back into shape and pretty soon the lid fitted and we were ready to get going.

CHARLEY: The heat was all but unbearable. We couldn't ride like this - tomorrow we needed to be away at first light and when the sun was at its highest we had to be off the bikes and in the shade drinking plenty of water.

EWAN: The road was much nastier than before. It rattled bones; my legs were aching, my arms, the small of my back. I was being battered around like a football. Fuck this road, it was like being on corrugated iron. I was puffing and panting, so hot I couldn't believe it.

CHARLEY: I saw Ewan in my mirrors bouncing around like a horseman trapped in a trot. That wasn't right; sweat was pouring off him, the bike smashing into the ruts so hard I could almost hear it.

Something was wrong.

He pulled up and we took a look at the back of his BMW.

'Fuck it, Ewan,' I said. 'Your suspension is shot.'

We were in forty-eight degrees of heat, blazing sunshine by the side of the road and there was no sign of Claudio. He'd ridden on to set up a shot. Ewan was still inspecting the shock. 'It's completely collapsed,' he said. 'I can't ride like this, Charley. It'll wreck the bike.'

Ewan called on the phone, spoke to Jimmy Simak and told him what had happened. 'Tell him we've got a spare shock absorber,' I said.

'Spare?' He looked incredulous. 'You put one in?'

I nodded. 'Last minute. I don't know why. It's the original BMW, by the way. They're going to love this, aren't they?'

'Yeah, they are.'

He was right. We only changed the shocks in the first place because Ohlins had such a good reputation. Ewan told Jimmy where we were and we shifted the bikes to the shade of some rocks.

Claudio got back just as the trucks arrived.

EWAN: Charley's a star. He'd been brilliant all day; not worried about the pace we were travelling. I know he can ride three times as fast as me on this kind of stuff yet he pootles along, never making me feel like I'm not up to it. Not only that, he was fixing my bike. I could have done it – it was me who replaced the shock with the Ohlins in the first place. But it was like something off the Dakar, he and Jim attacking the thing like a pit crew.

With my bike sound again I rode the few kilometres to our camp site, a high plateau sheltered by a hill of black rock, lying in slabs like chunks of liquorice. The sand was a wonderful colour, a burnt yellow. Looking back I noticed Claudio lurching along as if his bike was about to fall over.

One glance at the back wheel told us all we needed to know. The second shock absorber to go and we had no more spares.

Russ clicked into gear; problem-solving is his forte and he's really good at it. We were still two hundred miles from Dongola. Russ was in his element, however, taking care of business.

'Right,' he said, off the phone momentarily. 'Claudio can ride in one of the cars. Charley, we get the weight off your bike and hope the suspension lasts. I've been on the phone for spares but we can't get them to Khartoum till Sunday and even then there'll be customs issues.' He scratched his head. 'I've not figured the details exactly yet because we can't get visas for anyone to fly in from London.'

'So what do we do?' I asked him.

'Don't know yet. I'm working on it with Lucy back at the office. Now,' he went on, 'Amir reckons we can get someone out here with a truck and load up Claudio's bike either tonight or tomorrow. I'll go with him and get that organised. We can get the bike to Khartoum or, if there's a problem with spares, all the way to the Ethiopian border. Is that all right with you, Ewan. You and Charley on your own with Clouds in the car?'

'It's fine with me,' I said.

'OK, good. We'll be back.' With that he and Amir – our Sudanese fixer – climbed into the Nissan and headed off down the basin.

I drilled some holes in my boots to try and reduce the heat. I was wearing solid off-road ones because I wanted the security after breaking my leg. When they were fully ventilated I climbed the hill.

I wanted some peace and quiet and I wanted to soak up the atmosphere. I love the desert; it's so beautiful and inspiring. When I made the crest I stared out towards the horizon. Breathtaking.

The sand drifted among volcanic boulders; a savage, staggering beauty, barren and uncompromising.

CHARLEY: Russ was coming back – headlights swept the desert floor. He and Amir had found a village and persuaded someone to come out with a truck.

'Now as far as spares are concerned,' he said, 'apparently people from Tanzania can fly into Khartoum, so we're getting someone from there to meet Robin.' Robin is one of our production co-ordinators. 'He's flying to Cairo with spare shocks and he can give them to our man from Tanzania. He can then fly them into Khartoum for us.'

'Fucking hell,' Ewan said. 'How did you organise that?'

'Lucy thought of it. Good old Luce.'

EWAN: That first day we'd only managed to get sixty miles south. The next day, once Claudio's bike had been shipped out, we put 120 under our belts and were completely wasted by the end of it.

Last night a couple of kids had ridden into the camp on a donkey carrying a spray of wild dates still green and hard, sweet enough but not how you eat them at Christmas. Today we'd passed kids who waved and shouted, all smiles and laughter. Everyone in this country had been so friendly; it was hard to conceive that such horrors as Darfur were occurring only a few hundred miles north-west.

Left: Charley meets some Sudanese locals.

We met a few cyclists on the road; a couple from Switzerland had joined us for lunch – Kurt and Dorothy. We had been amazed to learn they'd been on the road for nine years. They were only heading home now because the woman's parents were elderly and needed looking after. They'd met in 1994 on separate bike trips in Argentina, of all places.

They had just come from Ethiopia and told us we'd have to watch for kids chucking stones. We'd seen it here; now and then a bunch of kids would run into the road and lob the odd rock as we were passing.

Soon we were riding again – quite comfortably; then I heard a clunk from under the bike. My heart missed a beat. The next thing I knew the power dipped and the engine stopped.

CHARLEY: A rock had smashed the sensor that tells the bike when the side stand is down. It's a safety device and as soon as you engage a gear the bike stops. With the sensor smashed the computer thought the stand was down.

The bike would start in neutral but if Ewan stepped on the gear lever it died. We looked to see if there was a connection we could undo, tracing cable up towards the engine until we found one. Ewan uncoupled it and tried the bike; it started fine but again died as soon as he put it in gear.

Neither of us was sure what to do. There was no shade here and it was blistering.

We called Steve, our mate from BMW in the UK. He was on his way to work and Ewan explained the situation. After a brief discussion Ewan hung up, then he cut the sensor off completely, stripped the cabling and exposed the wires. Red, white and brown, he twisted them together.

But the bike still wouldn't go.

We went back to Steve. He was at work now with another GS1200 in front of him and trying to figure out why it wouldn't work. Meanwhile we were at the side of the road in Sudan. Crazy, as mad as Russ calling the RAC from Libya.

While Steve was mulling it over I suggested to Ewan that maybe the brown wire was an earth and it was only the red and white we needed to twist. He was up for giving that a go but I was worried we might short the computer so we waited for Steve to call back. When he did he told us to twist just the red and white wires together. It used to be all three, he said, but now the brown was only an earth.

Bingo. Wires twisted and we were off and running.

EWAN: Thank God for that. And an hour or so later, after a sudden abundance of palm trees, we were at the river.

'Charley,' I said. 'Do you realise you've ridden your motorbike all the way from John O'Groats to the Nile? What do you think about that?'

'Fucking stupid. What do we want to do that for?'

He started singing Madness songs and I gazed across the water to where an old fort dominated the headland. It looked like something from the time of Christ.

Below: Jason Lewis had been on the road under his own steam for an amazing thirteen years.

'Can you see any crocs?' I said. 'This river's supposed to be teeming with them.'

Charley shaded his eyes from the sun. 'Why don't you throw yourself in and find out?'

Just love him, don't you?

We stopped for lunch in a town called Kerma, where kids were unloading melons from a donkey cart and old men sat in the shade drinking water from massive urns placed beneath the trees. We ate rice and vegetables with a bean curry.

The Swiss couple weren't the only people we met; the coolest thing had been early yesterday. We were riding along the dirt road in the middle of the desert when up ahead we saw a cyclist approaching, towing a little trailer. Charley pulled over. The guy just cycled up, nonchalant as you like. 'Mr McGregor, I presume,' he said.

Charley told him he'd got us mixed up, but the guy'd been on the road thirteen years so you can hardly blame him. His name was Jason Lewis and he'd left Greenwich in 1994 – just when the Swiss couple were meeting for the first time. He was on his way around the world using human power only. He'd had a mate with him to begin with but he bailed out in Hawaii. They'd crossed the Atlantic in a pedal boat, then the USA on roller blades and another pedal boat to cross the Pacific. Right now Jason was heading for Wozzi hazzer and the lake. If he got permission he planned to kayak all the way to Aswan. It was amazing really, thirteen years – a record among the road-weary we'd met to date.

CHARLEY: Dongola was a sandy town with wide streets and single storey buildings. I was following my nose – the smell of the river – and we came to the quay where cars were lined up waiting for the ferry. The boat was midstream and we parked alongside old Peugeots and battered pickups to wait. Everyone was dressed in white, most wearing turbans, drivers squatting at the edge of the water.

We met a lad from England, Tom Wilson, who'd been working his way north from Cape Town. He filmed us leaving the boat and riding up to the heaving market where people and cars, donkeys and camels mingled in one monstrous mêlée.

EWAN: That night we camped on what looked like moon rock or the ocean bed, a dune of pebbles sheltering us from the road and nothing to break up our horizon but the bikes and setting sun.

We spoke to the others, still on the road and about to stop for the night. We needed petrol and we'd hook up with them in the morning. I really admired people like Tom, Dave and Amelia; people who took off on their own with no satellite phone or back-up and no one to call when they met trouble.

We met Amelia and Dave, backpackers on their way to volunteer in Darfur, and really admired their sense of adventure.

The following morning we were back on shiny black tarmac. Yee-haw! I loved it. The desert was so varied and here it was yellow with a sort of burnt crust. We slowed to a stop as a herd of camels ambled across the scrub, the last one ridden by the herder, an elegant man in a white cap, sitting almost side-saddle with a quirt in his hand, looking as if he could have come from any period in history, nothing beyond him but desert.

We found Ad Baba a little further on, another small Sudanese town with sand roads and square buildings; houses, shops, people milling around and children waving and smiling. The children were incredible. I thought back to the other day when Charley and I stopped for lunch and one little boy came up to me. Taking my hand he held it all the time he spoke to me. I didn't understand him, but he didn't realise and he chatted away wide-eyed and all the time kept his wee hand in mine.

I managed to get him to tell a man who spoke some English what he was trying to tell me, and the man explained he just wanted me to know his name and where he lived, basically who he was.

It was a special moment. It reminded me how much I missed my own three girls.

CHARLEY: Sometimes I think we forget how lucky we are. For the people out here a twenty-nine-hour bus ride at ten miles an hour, sitting on hard metal benches while others squat among your luggage on the roof, is normal.

We were on tarmac now, eating up the miles and we saw a few of those big buses, crammed to the rafters. We also saw a lorry with a bunch of people sitting on the roof of the cab, their legs dangling in front of the windscreen. Imagine the driver braking hard – made me shudder just to think about it.

Past lunchtime and we came to Abu Dom – an everlasting town that seemed to go on and on; cars, vans and buses all jammed together. I asked a tuk-tuk driver the way – but in the end we were pulling up at junctions and yelling at drivers, 'Khartoum? Khartoum?'

As we came into Khartoum I noticed much newer cars and decent looking buildings, green spaces, walled gardens and parks even – and a lot of construction.

We crossed the Nile on an old iron bridge with a soldier watching from a shelter beside the road – just sitting there with his 50-calibre machine gun, chilling out in the shade.

The deeper we got into the capital the more excited I became. Ewan was full of it; the traffic, the roundabouts, the crazy mad junctions when the world and his wife seemed to be coming at you. Thank God for the traffic cops in white uniforms perched on their little islands.

The skyline was dominated by a weird looking white building with mirrored glass – the Al-Fatih Hotel. It turned out we were staying in a hotel next door. We parked the bikes and hauled our gear off. Ewan said he smelled like a badger's arse and went off to have a shower.

13

ETHIOPIA

KALASHNIKOVS & CUSTOMS

EWAN: After a week in Sudan the sound of rain rattling my tent was amazing: rain after so long, rain so heavy it would churn the ground into mush.

We'd rolled out of Khartoum around two in the afternoon, the sweat sticking to me. Even on open road at sixty miles an hour the wind was on fire.

Three hundred and fifty miles to the border.

CHARLEY: My hands were hurting: the injuries from Dakar. There's a nub of bone sticking down where I broke my left wrist. The surgeon welded it that way so I could ride a motorbike. It's fine most of the time but constant riding and it really begins to ache. On top of that the muscle at the base of my other hand sort of seizes up and every now and then I have to reach across with my left to use the throttle.

The weirdest thing, though, is how I have so little strength in the ends of my fingers: it makes things like doing up buttons, or undoing my wife's bra, really awkward.

We were travelling south-east towards Gedaref, the road straight and dusty, full of mad bus drivers and road trains. The scenery wasn't much to look at until we came to an aeroplane graveyard. You know, like the proverbial elephant's graveyard only this one had planes in it. There were loads of ancient heaps; the fuselages intact but the wings peeling in strips that fluttered in the wind.

Amazingly we found a whole community living there; they had little shacks dotted among the old aircraft. It was surreal: all these dead aeroplanes and a group of men sitting round a fire brewing tea. We shook hands and went back to the bikes.

It struck me more forcefully than ever how so much of the world is nothing like what we're used to in the West. Most people live way below the poverty line. The things we take for granted just don't figure in their lives.

EWAN: We rode into the darkness and the desert. Hardcore camping, just the two of us, fantastic, and we were up with the sun. The land was greener now with more hills, more trees. A troop of baboons crossed the road right in front of me. Now I knew we were heading south.

As we approached the border the country was greener still. I could see a metal arch ahead and a herd of goats crossing. We left Sudan and I could see the Ethiopian flag – red, green and yellow – and above it someone had erected a banner: 'Welcome to Ethiopia Charley Boorman, Ewan McGregor and the Long Way Down team'.

Perfect, I thought. I might have to talk to my agent about that billing, though.

Across Africa we ran into plenty of geep (as we called them), a sort of cross between a sheep and a goat.

As with every border everything suddenly changed – there was the smell of rain in the air, everywhere was green. The town was heaving with people, on foot or riding donkeys or on carts drawn by donkeys. The houses and shops were higgledy-piggledy and hunched together as if that was the only way they'd stay standing. They were made of everything you could imagine and painted in bright green, purple and red. The whole place was vibrant, a real frontier town.

I realised that Sudan had been the colour of sand; everyone wore white and whenever we'd stopped it was only the men who'd come over. It was an Islamic state and the women were very much in the background. Here everyone came to see us: men, women, young boys and girls; the place had a tangibly freer feel to it.

At passport control – a mud hut painted green and purple – I shook hands with Charley. 'Well, mate, here we are. We crossed the desert. Can you believe it? We crossed the fucking desert!'

And now it was night and hammering down with rain. What I've not mentioned yet is that we were thirty kilometres from the border in a compound enclosed by barbed wire with three Kalashnikov-toting guards on the gate.

Getting through immigration had been so easy that David had tempted fate: 'This could be real quick guys.'

And were about to get going when our Ethiopian fixer, Habtamu, explained that we'd been assigned an armed guard. He accompanied us to the next village and the customs compound which of course, was closing. But they'd seen how detailed our carnets were and told us they wanted to make a thorough examination of our gear. Everything would have to come off the trucks – tomorrow. So that was it, our first night in Ethiopia courtesy of customs men and Kalashnikovs.

14.

ETHIOPIA

A CUP OF GINGER TEA

CHARLEY: We were up at six and gone by ten – the usual four hours. The guard, the gun-for-hire, stayed with the support crew. Apparently travellers needed an armed escort as far as Gonder.

We went on ahead. I couldn't get over how different Ethiopia was – it had rained all night. Sudan had been dry and empty; this was mountainous, much cooler, with everyone on the street.

The rain stopped, but the cloud hung like a fog as we headed for the Eritrean border. We were on a high plateau, the land green and cultivated. I could see farmers on their terraces trailing ancient hand ploughs behind teams of skinny oxen.

It was June and the rainy season was supposed to start at the end of the month but already we'd seen the first signs.

EWAN: A completely different world. We passed herders ushering donkeys laden with goods, donkeys that wandered all over the road. Kids would pop up from nowhere with their hands out: 'You, you!' they were yelling. Big kids, little kids, tiny boys with shaved heads and top knots, little girls in scruffy dresses, bare feet and shawls.

I was uplifted. The desert had dried me out, now I felt invigorated.

We stopped in Gonder for a lunch of cake, coke and coffee. Gonder is the regional capital, a bustling town. A group of teenagers descended on us and one wee man in a striped T-shirt recognised me.

'You make movies?' he said in English.

'Yeah.'

'Why don't you arrive in a big car? Why did you arrive on a motorbike?'

'Because I'm doing a motorbike programme.'

'Ah,' he said. 'Do you have a bodyguard?'

I held up all of my fingers. 'I have ten,' I told him, then pointed to the rooftops, 'all around, so be careful.'

CHARLEY: The clouds swept in low and dull and it was suddenly misty. We passed stands of eucalyptus and acacias. This was a poor country, I knew, but the land was tilled in terraces and the soil obviously rich – it was that dark moist colour, such a contrast to the sand of Sudan.

We kept stopping for livestock, the road blocked by sheep with fat tails, little goats, or skinny cattle. The higher we got the more the clouds swamped us and it got cold. We passed a mass migration of people all wearing the same colour shawls and driving their animals ahead of them.

The road was muddy, pot-holed and littered with puddles. We picked our way carefully and found a campsite that was sheltered by eucalyptus.

With David and Russ – supporting us all the way.

There were three children at first, three girls wearing long dresses with shawls round their heads. They were quiet initially but as Ewan's jokes got worse, they grew bolder.

One little thing with a gap in her teeth was the cheekiest by far. We nicknamed her Ruby, because in a funny way she reminded Ewan of Ruby Wax. We gave them water and they loved the plastic bottles. We passed out the empties we were carrying. The three became four, five, six, then seven and so on. I noticed that each one who arrived was a little older, a little bigger. They crowded around us. We heard the first rumble of thunder and I knew we were in for another downpour; two wet nights in a row, it was so strange after the heat of Sudan.

The children were fascinated by the camera; they kept running right up to the lens and blowing raspberries on the backs of their hands.

Eventually a man appeared, tall and elegant. He was the father of some of them, certainly, and he ushered them off home.

Only now did we think about food. We ate boil-in-the-bag, standing by the bikes, head torches on as the clouds rolled in.

EWAN: It rained all night but was clear again in the morning. Up at dawn we wandered across the hill and a field of rocks where cattle were grazing and sheep skipped out of our way. We wanted to see where the kids lived and came across a cluster of huts anyway. These were pole-walled; the gaps filled with wattle and daub and the roofs thatched. We saw little Ruby first and she was all giggles and laughter. Her family invited us in for breakfast. There were two women, who we guessed were Ruby's mother and

grandmother, and a guy in a blue jacket, wellies and a scarf. He was the head man and we recognised him from the night before. He sat down on a canvas bench, ushering Charley and me to take a seat while the older woman ground some kind of root on a smooth stone.

There was a little fire going, the circular room dark, though with the door open and the windows there was enough light to make out a zigzag pattern on the walls and hand prints made by the children. Shelves had been cut and held various pots. Charley pointed out beams in the roof, blackened from a thousand fires.

The root smelled of ginger, and once it was mashed the older woman (who kept smiling and laughing) added it to water she was heating in an ancient black kettle. Ruby came in with a chipped basin and some water and we washed our hands. Her father set down a plate of sour bread together with a spicy garlic paste and indicated for us to dig in.

All the time we were eating a cow stood at the window, dogs barked outside and every now and again a cock crowed. It was very peaceful; the family so gracious and generous. We'd arrived unannounced and they just opened their home.

The tea was superb; the old lady served us in tall glasses and with the bread and spicy paste it was a good breakfast. A family in Ethiopia: this was why we were here, to meet the people, see how they lived and share a meal with them.

CHARLEY: The paste blew my mouth off and I almost spilled the basin of water. The people were lovely, though, and their home beautiful. They had newspaper cuttings on the walls and religious pictures, icons: this was predominantly a Christian country with only about 30 per cent of the people Muslim, and they tended to live more to the east, nearer Eritrea and the Afar Depression.

The little walkways between the huts and the enclosures for animals were puddle-strewn and daubed with animal dung. The kids were barefoot, their feet and legs streaked with filth and one or two had gummy eyes. These were very poor but very proud, very hospitable people. We said goodbye, slipped the father some money for our food and went back to the bikes.

When we got there we found Claudio's jacket was gone. Ewan and I had been wearing ours but he'd left his draped over the tank bag and someone had stolen it. It put a bit of a damper on what had been a special morning.

We rode on, climbing higher and closing on the Simien National Park. I was behind Ewan when we came to a bunch of kids. They waved at first as they always do, but then they bent for stones.

'Oi!' I yelled. 'Oi!' I lifted a finger, looking back sharply.

We rode ever higher, in open upland, the clouds so low we rode right into them. Through another town and saw what looked like a bunch of prisoners; men dressed the

same and breaking a pile of massive rocks with sledgehammers. There were a number of other guys standing there with these great poles. They looked weird, three abreast, the poles upright like lances.

We were heading into the Simien Mountains to see the Gelada baboons we'd seen on David Attenborough's *Planet Earth*. And this was some of the most spectacular scenery I've ever seen; gently rolling hills, only you were twelve thousand feet up. The roads got narrower, tighter and twistier – the mountains shouldered one side and the drop would kill you on the other.

Rounding one final bend the baboons crossed the road in front of us. There were tons of them; long-haired and totally unafraid of people, they were all across the mountain. Parking up we sat down and watched them.

'I can't believe it,' Ewan said. 'I mean, you see them on *Planet Earth* and there they are.'

'And the view,' I said. 'What do you think of the view?'

'Amazing: the clouds, like smoke over the mountains.'

'Yeah, bloody smoke machine . . .'

The view was staggering: mountains that stretched for mile after mile, valleys between them, canyons and gorges green with trees and grey with rock, thousands of feet below. We wandered right to the edge of one drop, the land falling away at our feet.

'How about camping down there?' I said. 'A ledge or a tree, maybe; you know, strap yourself in and watch the sunset.'

'Fine,' Ewan stated. 'I'll watch you from up here.'

EWAN: I kept thinking about the children, no shoes, scabs everywhere, running eyes and shit all over their feet.

Claudio's jacket had been a bummer but I tried to focus on the positive – the family's hospitality, and the national park had been amazing. Some of the roads were pretty terrifying, though, especially on the way down. They were serious hairpins with a drop to nowhere: it made the hairs on your arse curl up. We stopped at one place where the fall was just ridiculous and Habtamu, our fixer, told us that when Ethiopia was under communist rule, the governor of the Gonder region used to bring dissidents up here and chuck them over the cliffs.

'Riding along I watched the different colours of the earth, thinking about how it changes so much, the yellow and black of Sudan to the green and brown of Ethiopia.' EWAN

15

ETHIOPIA

THE ROAD AT THE END
OF THE WORLD

CHARLEY: Kids were on the road all the time: tiny little things carrying huge jerricans, usually tied by a length of rope on their backs. Sometimes the nearest fresh water to where they live is a few miles walk and carrying water is a chore the children help with. It's one of the reasons some kids never make it to school. That and the firewood – we saw people gathering it all the time, old women bent double under huge bundles wrapped in calico cloth.

Kids popped up from all over; not just the villages, but the hillside, from great drops where the road bordered the gorges, they'd be on bridges, along the river beds . . . everywhere. Ninety per cent of them were terrific, all waves and smiles with just a handful who liked to wave sticks or pick up rocks.

We were descending again, on uncertain gravel, and taking a left hander when Ewan lost the front. It just washed away, no warning. He was off before he knew it and my heart was in my mouth.

By the time I pulled up he was already hefting the bike from the dirt. He didn't say anything, just took a look for damage and refixed the tank bag.

EWAN: I was used to the spills by now and what choice did I have? What was I going to do, leave the bike and hitch a lift?

Riding along I watched the different colours of the earth, thinking about how it changes so much, the yellow and black of Sudan to the green and brown of Ethiopia. On a motorcycle you really feel it, smell it – you're part of it. Every now and then you come into contact with it and it hurts. That's just the way it is.

We crossed rivers on bridges built by the Italian army back in the 1930s, passing cattle and sheep that were often just lying in the road. We were seeing a few camels now and hundreds of donkeys carrying everything you can imagine.

We were able to grab some lunch in Axum and a quick shower – it was a week since the last one – but we had to press on as the UNICEF team were waiting for us in Adigrat.

The route looked pretty gnarly in places, but I was in good spirits. I actually thought the riding was fantastic and we were heading towards the Eritrean border, which in itself was amazing. Travellers just don't go there.

For thirty years Eritrea and Ethiopia were at war with each other; Eritrea finally gaining independence in 1991. But between 1998 and 2000 the fighting flared up again over territorial demarcation lines. It was tragic, especially when you consider the countries share pretty much the same traditions and religious beliefs.

Anyway, that's where we were headed and the road was part dirt, part pothole and part sand. When it rained the tarmac part looked like a sheet of glass.

And boy did it rain. We were climbing to rugged, open plateaus with the most fantastic cloud-soaked mountains all around us. I could see bolts of lightning and thunder was crashing overhead. The raindrops were fucking monstrous, falling hard as hail, and in no time the world was running with water.

CHARLEY: The ride was fantastic, a mountain road in a thunderstorm. Fucking amazing! I could hear Ewan whooping it up over the radio; his being the only one that was transmitting now and, as it turned out, that was about to pack up.

Not before I heard his latest song, though; he makes them up as he's riding and this one went: 'Riding along in the pouring rain, think I might be quite insane'.

I loved this country, though it was a tough life for the people. But to ride through it was just incredible, beautiful.

It was dark when we arrived, but UNICEF had organised a small hotel in a gated compound where the bikes would be safe. The town was buzzing, a real border place full of soldiers, bomb disposal experts, truck drivers and the kind of professions that followed them.

Sarah and Wendy were waiting for us and it was great to see them. They introduced us to Indrias, the UNICEF communications officer who was to be our guide. He was Ethiopian but had been to school in Massachusetts and university in Philadelphia. He was based in Addis Ababa but worked a lot in Tigray region. Previously a journalist, he'd covered the Eritrean War.

The girls had been in touch with our families and brought out some food parcels, namely chocolate and sweeties. For Ewan there was also a photo of all of his girls, and for me pictures of Doone and Kinvara.

The following morning we were in the back of a UNICEF 4x4 heading for the border. Indrias sat between us and we talked about the country. He cited the successes UNICEF was having with education: these days 70 per cent of Ethiopian children are receiving at least primary education whereas just a few years ago the figure was only about 15 per cent.

Although AIDS is a huge issue, with one and a half million people infected, preventable diseases had been greatly reduced. Basic sanitation such as we'd seen in Kenya had brought the mortality rate among under-fives down significantly. Indrias told us that as recently as 2005 almost half a million under-fives were dying of things that could easily be prevented. In malaria-affected areas, twenty million nets were being distributed, although along some of the rivers the men used them for fishing. Dug latrines, washbasins and soap were preventing diarrhoea and therefore dysentery, another big killer. UNICEF was also drilling thousands of wells fitted with hand-pumps, just one of which could serve five hundred families.

We were about fifty kilometres from where the serious fighting had been and many of those displaced had fled to Adigrat. Technically there was no war any more but then there was no peace either. Indrias explained that the level of rhetoric had risen again recently and the people lived in a constant state of fear.

Most of the fighting had been from trenches, lines and lines of which were dug along the one thousand kilometre border. The casualty figures were staggering and the conflict had been compared to World War I.

Three hundred thousand people had been displaced, many of them Ethiopians deported from Eritrea who, when the ceasefire was declared, had no homes to go back to. The ones that did go home found their houses and watering holes were now in the middle of minefields.

Both sides used mines but at least the Ethiopian government was able to furnish the UN with maps. The Eritrean mines hadn't been mapped and over five hundred people have been injured in Tigray since 1998 – three hundred of them children – and a quarter of those died.

There are more than a million mines along the border and it costs three dollars to lay a landmine and $1,000 to destroy it. UNICEF estimates that more than two million Ethiopian children live in mine-affected areas.

EWAN: Indrias explained what steps UNICEF was taking to try to combat the risk. They'd initiated a Mine Risk Education Programme. Education (particularly for children) is the key and so far they had reached over two hundred thousand youngsters. As a result, 69 per cent of kids had altered their behaviour.

Charley sitting on an abandoned tank: a great big bit of machinery, slowly rusting away in the sand.

Tigray had been really successful but nevertheless huge numbers had sustained hideous injuries. UNICEF hopes to provide at least three thousand of the most badly injured with a new mobility cycle, one of which was on the roof of the truck ahead of us. Specifically designed with mine injuries and the tough terrain in mind, they're powered by hand pedals which work independently of one another. They can climb and descend, they have three gears and the difference they make to a child's independence is incalculable.

Indrias went on to explain that as part of its Mine Action advocacy work, UNICEF was calling on all countries not only to sign but also to ratify the Ottawa Treaty banning anti-personnel land mines. Ethiopia signed the treaty more than ten years ago but only ratified it in 2004. Countries such as the United States and China have yet to sign it.

It isn't easy to get countries to give them up, however, because landmines make the perfect guard. Trouble is, when the war is over the troops leave and the real victims start appearing. One wrong step and lives are either over or ruined. In this particular conflict mines were deliberately placed where civilians would come into contact with them: along river banks, for example, where water carriers or goat herders would get blown up; around the cactus plant that bears the prickly pear, a fruit often picked by children. Worst of all, though, were the ones deliberately planted on somebody's doorstep.

Opposite right:
Tesfu lost his leg when he stepped on a mine that had been buried on his doorstep. He was determined not to let it destroy his life.

We were in high desert now having climbed beyond rivers where we saw women washing clothes, people taking baths, other people washing buses. The terrain was barren and sand coloured, though the fields were cultivated; we watched men with oxen and hand ploughs tilling the soil in the same way they'd been doing for a thousand years.

Off-road we headed for Addis Tesfa, a small sandstone village of low walls and cacti. There was a desolate beauty to it – kids running around barefoot, donkeys wandering here and there, and of course the skinny but beautiful cattle. With their huge horns and soft eyes they reminded me of drawings we'd seen on tombs in the Valley of the Kings.

We had come to see a guy called Tesfu. He was twenty years old, slightly built with cropped hair and a pencil-line moustache.

Six years ago he lost his right leg to a mine.

Shaking hands he showed me and Charley to a bench that ran along the wall outside his house. He spoke little English and Indrias interpreted.

Tesfu had been a bright student and had got as far as the equivalent American eighth grade, but because of his injuries he'd had to drop out of school. Even now, almost 85 per cent of Ethiopians are illiterate and Tesfu is acutely aware that education is the key to his future.

His voice had a gentle timbre and he was a guy who used to love running and playing football. When war came he and his family fled to Adigrat where they stayed for two years. When it was deemed safe to go home they found their house all but ruined and that same day started building a new one. The old house had been on the other side of the courtyard from where we were sitting. They'd been back a couple of days when, one afternoon, Tesfu was by himself and went inside to get something. The mine had been laid right outside the door.

He was fourteen years old. Four days later he regained consciousness with one leg missing below the knee and the other a mass of shrapnel slivers.

He has a prosthetic leg now but it was a bit knackered. It was held above his knee with a strap and the foot was actually broken. But it was better than nothing and he didn't want to use one of the new cycles even though once trained he could then train others and UNICEF would pay him. He needs an income, but emotionally he says the last thing he can deal with is a wheelchair: he's young, male and proud, and who can blame him.

He really wants to be a doctor, because doctors saved his life and he wants to save other lives. The problem is school, because the nearest one is a three kilometre walk and he can't make it. The wound where they tidied up his leg wasn't brilliant, apparently, and it gave him a lot of pain. A better prosthesis is what he needs, but the real pain actually came from the shrapnel still embedded in his other leg. He showed us a hole in his kneecap where the skin is stretched and white from scarring. His body is apparently repelling the shrapnel and they can't operate right away. Tesfu told us that perhaps something can be done but he has no idea when. In the meantime he's doing all he can with massage and a traditional healer.

CHARLEY: He was a brave kid and he desperately wanted to finish his education. He told us he was unlucky and yet lucky, God had saved his life. He wanted his independence and he was active in helping educate other children about the dangers of mines. I really admired him and I was disgusted by the cruelty he'd been subjected to. I couldn't get my head round a person who'd place a landmine on a doorstep, a deliberate act to fuck someone up.

Tesfu went with us to Addis Alem, where we were greeted by a procession of school children. The flags were flying and a banner had been put up proclaiming a welcome to Ewan and Charley. Talk about humbling: there were hundreds of kids, all clapping their hands and singing a song of welcome.

We got a fantastic warm welcome at Addis Alem.

The first of the mobility cycles had been delivered to a fifteen-year-old girl called Abrehet. Three years ago she was walking home from school when she stepped on a mine. The blast blew off one leg and ripped the flesh from the other leaving just the bone. It meant she couldn't walk with any kind of crutch. She could handle the bike, though, and seemed pretty proud of the fact.

She led the procession down to the school buildings where the children were going to show us one of the plays they'd devised specifically to educate other children about mines. Abrehet was one of the first people in Ethiopia to receive the mobility cycle and after only three days she was using the controls to go forwards, back up, brake and turn circles; she gave us quite a performance. I reckon we were there for an hour or so and the smile never left her face.

Abrehet was a real inspiration: at just fifteen she was independent, full of courage and had great plans for her future, despite the terrible injuries she's sustained from a mine.

Thousands of mines were laid in this area during the war between Ethiopia and Eritrea. Here we are being shown the incredibly dangerous and painstaking task of de-mining a small patch of ground.

Ironically it was watching her that changed Tesfu's mind; having seen the bike in action he realised that it was actually quite cool, and by the time we left he'd told Indrias and Ewan that he'd like one. It was brilliant: now he had a way of getting to school, and with school he had a future.

We were told that Abrehet received nine hundred *birr* – around $100 – as compensation from the government, and she'd used it to buy eleven goats. Her favourite subject at school was social studies and she wanted to become a businesswoman. By my reckoning she was well on her way – a year after she bought the goats the eleven had become nineteen.

Welcoming us, the head teacher told us a little bit about the area and Ewan and I were appalled when he explained that forty-eight people had been killed by mines and another 127 injured.

He spoke about the challenges the community had overcome and those they were still facing. He told us that the immediate area had been cleared and they had found a staggering 3576 mines.

We were then introduced to Daniel, a young guy who cleared mines for the UN. He showed us how he located them and just how long it took.

First, however, he showed us the mines themselves. There was one in particular, Jesus Christ; it looked like a bit of wood some kid would pick up for the fire. Daniel told us it was an RGD6 and came from the old USSR; the cover was wooden and it contained four hundred grammes of TNT.

Three dollars to lay a mine, remember, and $1,000 – not to mention the decades it takes – to get rid of them.

That's what Daniel does. Dressed in a chest plate, protective helmet and knee pads, he uses a piece of wood that's about a metre in length. It's painted red and coiled with string at both ends. The other end of the string is tied to a couple of rocks and with this contraption he forms a pathway through a minefield.

He uses a mine detector (like a long handled metal detector) and if it throws up a sound he marks the spot with a stone which later he sprays with yellow or red paint. Then he's on his knees and using his prodder, a metal spike on a plastic handle. He very slowly digs around the area. It's painstaking work, not to mention incredibly stressful. If it is a mine he will either render it safe or – if he thinks it's booby trapped – blow it up in situ, using a shaped charge or a hook and line. This is tough manual work and takes amazing patience. If Daniel is lucky he can clear a metre of ground in a day.

EWAN: The children acted out a scene from a hillside where two young lads were herding some cattle. It was very funny at first, the boys beating the cattle (two other kids wearing animal skins) with sticks, when along came a bloke carrying a sack and yelling out like a rag and bone man. Apparently there were peddlers who travelled around the area buying up old bits of metal, which they sold on to blacksmiths in the bigger towns.

The children know they can get money for any metal they find; the trouble is most of the fragments are left over from the war. Anyway, the metal-peddler was chatting to the kids when one hurried off to find something he'd spotted earlier.

It was a fuse and the mine went up. It was very dramatic. The boy made it look as though his arm had been blown off and was rolling around, screaming. The other kids backed off immediately. The extent of his plight was really brought home when I realised no one could get to him. An injured child in agony, perhaps bleeding to death and no one could get to him. The whole area could be mined and there was nothing anyone could do except get hold of someone like Daniel.

We were due to go on to Zelambassa, but still had one last privilege to perform in Addis Alem. The name translates as New World and that is fitting because in Ethiopia the year is 1999. They use the Julian calendar and their millennium is ushered in on 12 September. Indrias told us that as part of their millennium celebrations the country is planting sixty million trees, twenty million by school children.

A hundred years ago, 40 per cent of the country was covered with trees, today it's less than 3 per cent and they're cutting down more trees than they're planting. On top of that the most prevalent tree is the eucalyptus; it's not indigenous, its roots spread disproportionately, and it sucks up all the nutrients in the ground. When the kids were asked what they wanted to do to mark the millennium they came up with the idea of trees to make sure their country had a viable environment for the future.

We were each given a native cedar sapling. There was a mantra: 'Plant a tree, protect yourself, and protect Ethiopia's future.'

CHARLEY: This was the third such visit we'd made since we left John O'Groats and it was hugely inspiring to see what one human being can do for another, especially when set against the backdrop of what one human being can do to another.

Ewan was especially thoughtful. He's not mentioned it but only yesterday we'd heard about William. We'd met him at Robin House, the children's hospice in Scotland, just over a month ago, and his ambition had always been to meet Ewan. A few days after he achieved that ambition he passed away. It was very sad news and our hearts went out to his family.

The news reminded us that much of what we're doing is about awareness; it's about raising the profile of these places so UNICEF can go on with its mine education programme, Riders for Health can make sure AIDS victims survive and CHAS can continue creating memories.

Leaving Addis Alem we headed for the border town of Zelambassa. The reception blew me away. It seemed as if the whole town had turned out. Seven years ago Zelambassa had been at the forefront of the fighting and had been evacuated. The Eritrean forces razed it to the ground. It has only been partially rebuilt, bomb-blasted buildings line the streets and the only roofs are made of tin and have been provided by UNICEF.

The noise was incredible; women creating a high pitched, shrill sort of shrieking led by one woman with a microphone plugged into a bullhorn. She took us through the battered streets; a war zone still and the only one I'd witnessed first hand. We were surrounded by crowds of men and women wearing their traditional shawls, the gabbi and the netella. Most people carried umbrellas, all different shapes and sizes, to protect them from the sun, and they congregated in two shattered buildings. They perched everywhere: on piles of rubble, concrete blocks, the upper floors where the roofs had been blown off; they sat on steps, half-ruined walls . . . everywhere we looked, there were people gathering round us.

The district officer spoke for a few moments then Ewan and I thanked the town for such amazing hospitality, people with so little giving so much. An elder got to his feet, a gentle and intelligent looking man. He explained that Zelambassa had been a bustling place, a centre of commerce and trade and yet after seven years it still looked like this. He said the people had a strong bond with UNICEF, who had provided essential services. He said visitors were always welcome and the people appreciated those groups who were helping them. He was proud of his town; it had been a big town, a well known town before it had been destroyed. He said that people were still suffering. Countless had been injured by mines.

He told us that Eritrea had agreed to pay compensation but no monies had as yet been forthcoming. There was support from the Ethiopian government but so far only those who owned their own homes had received help. Not all the schools had been rebuilt and not all the health facilities; there was a shortage of basic essentials. He thanked us for coming and thanked UNICEF and all the agencies who'd remembered Zelambassa. But he asked us not to forget that the problems still went on.

He sat down and we were about to walk up to the border when another old man spoke up.

'Don't rush off,' he said. 'We have lots of problems we want to tell you.'

A UNICEF official explained that Ewan and I weren't from an agency and though we could raise awareness there was little we could do personally about specific situations.

As we walked to the front line a young policeman, who'd previously been in the army, told me this was the road at the end of the world. The road no longer went anywhere and so many people still lacked the most fundamental things like shelter, food and clean water. He said the people didn't understand who we were but knew we were from the West and they hoped we could help. He doubted many westerners had even heard of Zelambassa. Maybe we could tell them.

We were lucky enough to have coffee prepared for us the Ethiopian way,
with the beans roasted right there and then.

EWAN: We ate *injera*, the traditional Ethiopian dish that's made from a millet pancake,
with goat's meat and lamb curry, or the vegetables people eat on official fast days. A
woman made coffee with a charcoal stove on the floor, grinding the beans in front of us
whilst seated on a carpet of grass. This is long-established Ethiopian hospitality and
riding through some of the river deltas we'd seen women gathering grass for just such
occasions. The fire is laced with frankincense bark and the smell is amazing.

Charley and I sat with Tesfu and Luam, another amputee, a beautiful young girl
wearing a red netella and a flip-flop as part of her prosthetic foot. Mines ensure there's
never any peace. They devastate lives. Both Charley and I are absolutely convinced that
there should be a blanket ban on their use. So on behalf of Tesfu, Abrehet and Luam; on
behalf of every child who has lost a limb or lost their life to these grisliest of weapons,
we're calling on every country that makes, sells or uses land mines to stop.

Simple humanity, isn't it?

‘I was knackered and my concentration was slipping. We were on a much more gnarly stretch of road now, heading into the mountains and the town of Kembolcha. I was exhausted.’ EWAN

16

ETHIOPIA & KENYA

SAND, SORROW & CEREMONY

CHARLEY: I had three nails in my back tyre. Pulling them out I plugged the holes with rubber and cement, the same kind of kit I'd used on Claudio's bike when we made Long Way Round and he'd got all the way across Russia without incident.

Coming down from Adigrat we were into scrub desert, with sand edging the road. The towns looked more prosperous, built of brick or stone and painted in bright colours. Mkele was not far, the capital of Tigray region, and beyond that Maychew and eventually Addis.

EWAN: I was feeling good. Yesterday at Zelambassa was special and I won't forget it.

Today the road wasn't bad, though there were loads of children, of course. One boy started after us. 'Give me pen,' he was yelling. 'Escrito, escrito.' There's still quite an Italian influence here leftover from the days of occupation. The boy just wouldn't quit and pretty soon he was joined by another child and another until a whole tribe was tearing after the bikes. There were more on the hillside, a couple on the roof of a house. Claudio was filming from the back of Charley's bike and as we sped off he felt a stone thwack his helmet.

Later, coming down into the twisty stuff – hairpin city – my bike didn't feel good, felt loose and seemed to load up, almost weave, as I took the corners. I was saying as much on the video diary. Avoiding a lorry and sand on the road, I peeled into a left hand hairpin.

Shit, I'm down.

I was on my side, the bike sliding away and pirouetting on the tarmac. Kind of cool, actually, my helmet cam kept filming and, watching the footage later, it was like something off Moto GP.

The bike weighed a ton and the horn was blaring. I managed to wheel it to the side of the road and a few minutes later Charley was back. We checked for damage: the pannier was scraped and one of the bags on the crash bars but that was about it.

'There's oil on the front tyre.' Charley bent to show me. 'You picked up some oil, Ewan, it's why the front washed out. Are you all right?'

'I'm fine.'

Moving to the wall we took a look at the view across the valley.

'What's that big town down there?' Charley pointed.

'Birmingham.'

We laughed.

'Did you see that truck back there?' I asked him.

'You mean the one that missed the bend?' We'd seen it earlier. A lorry had dived over the edge. It was in two pieces, the cab smashed to bits on the section of road below. Debris was littered all across the carriageway. God knows how long it had been there.

A reminder that tarmac could be even more dangerous than going off-road.

CHARLEY: In Maychew we stopped for petrol and a cup of coffee. Ewan went to buy some food for dinner and I videoed a few kids then showed them the footage on my handlebar screen.

I grabbed a coffee in the cafe, sitting on the veranda where the kids were ushered away by the older men. When Ewan got back I gave the waiter ten *birr* and he gave me seven back. I looked surprised.

'No, no, it was only three,' he said.

I hadn't got a clue how much the coffee was but was really impressed by such honesty, particularly when you consider these people have so little.

We crossed a huge valley with mountains rising in the distance. We passed one town where we were sure we saw a dead guy. He lay awkwardly on the ground and he wasn't moving. He had a rope tied round his neck and a whole group of men were gathered around him.

We didn't stop.

By midday I was ragged; I'd noticed recently that by eleven or twelve I was exhausted. We really needed the few days we were taking at Addis Ababa.

EWAN: I was knackered and my concentration was slipping. We were on a much more gnarly stretch of road now, heading into the mountains and the town of Kembolcha. I was exhausted and there were geep all over the road. That's what I christened the sort of sheep/goat or goat/sheep animals we kept seeing. They wandered along as if they were permanently in the rain: heads down, jaw dragging, their fatty tails just hanging. They had this habit of drifting across the road, finding their mates, then all of them would lie down together for a kip.

The road was awful, blind hairpins with no run off and crazy drops down the mountain. Stones and gravel, dust, rock slides – the works.

I came off again. Going too fast, too confident, I don't know, but the next thing I knew I was slammed on my side.

My pride isn't bomb proof and I could see with this trip it would take another battering. It's a shame, because I get sick of off-road riders coming up to me in restaurants, looking smug and telling me I fall off all the time. Maybe I do, I don't know; maybe I'm just not very good at this. It's true that at the moment I'm not getting any pleasure from riding in the dirt. But I reckon I've been riding for fifty days now, half of them off-road, and I imagine even the most ardent dirt bikers would fall off a few times if they rode solidly for twenty-five days.

EWAN: We were approaching the Kenyan border now and our last few days in Ethiopia were pretty eventful. Before we got to Addis we visited the market at Bati and had been absolutely mobbed. There were hundreds of little kids all over us as soon as we pulled up. They were chased off by bigger kids who were in turn chased off by even bigger kids with long sticks. Finally surrounded by self-appointed bodyguards, Charley and I wandered among stalls selling everything from cloth to spice to live chickens and chewable roots with hallucinogenic properties. We saw tall, thin men with afro hair that had been lacquered until it looked wet. Women keeping the sun off with umbrellas sold millet and maize, donkeys, geep and camels. Legs tied together, the geep were tossed on top of buses to be transported. Across the way from the livestock, black-winged vultures sat watchfully in trees, waiting for the carcasses of the weakest to be tossed over the fence.

Beyond the Kenya border we had armed guards with us – four soldiers appointed by the government. This was a dangerous area, with clan warfare, poaching and banditry. 'Shiftas' operated here, and they liked to target anyone who looked like a tourist. They were particularly busy around the border and our fixer suggested we crack on to a lodge five hours drive away.

We'd been travelling maybe forty-five minutes when Claudio's suspension exploded. We couldn't believe it; the shock absorber had only just been fitted in Sudan. Fortunately we had spares we'd picked up in Addis, so Charley and I set about replacing it. Fitted in fifty minutes. Not bad for the side of a dirt road with shiftas looking on from the hills.

And talking of shiftas it was getting late and there was no way we'd make the lodge before dark. The fixer knew a place, though he didn't seem delighted about it – but we did have four Kalashnikovs to fall back on.

CHARLEY: In the morning we were off early and heading south-west on decent gravel. Ewan did really well, riding with his elbows out, soft hands and leaning back. He'd had a hard time in Ethiopia and coped brilliantly, now I got the feeling things would click.

The road was wide red gravel; it blended into the landscape, lots of bushes and very few trees – the African prairie.

It was hard to believe the atrocities that had been carried out at Turbi Primary School but the pupils there were determined to stay in school and think of their future.

We came to the Gabran people's village of Turbi. We'd read about it, seen it on BBC news and our mood sobered considerably. A clutch of buildings surrounding a sun-baked yard, we parked the bikes in the shade of acacia and took off our helmets. Immediately we were mobbed by children of all ages in pale blue shirts and green shorts. This was the school where two years previously twenty-two children had been massacred. Their head teacher Gabriel came over and we shook hands, told him who we were and that we'd heard about the atrocity.

He was in his forties, well spoken, and it was obvious he was the pillar around which the community had rebuilt itself. He told us he had no real idea why such things happened, but the disputes over land, pasture and water for animals went back generations.

It had been six o'clock in the morning, the children in school, when men from the neighbouring Borona clan opened fire.

'I saw men in uniform,' Gabriel told us. 'They just started shooting and they were still far away. I shouted to the children. Run. Run. Run.' He shook his head. 'The older ones, most of them were nine or ten, they understood the danger. But the young ones, they just stood there.' He pointed to the open ground between the buildings where the children were playing. 'They were cut down, slaughtered; the young ones, the babies. Not with guns, with knives, machetes.'

EWAN: It was horrific, incomprehensible, the kids, the little totty ones just standing there in bewilderment. Moments later, they were hacked to pieces.

'There was nothing we could do. They just died,' Gabriel said. 'They just died while we were watching.'

I remembered the BBC news reports when it had happened. Incredibly distressing, yet the place seemed to have recovered: clearly this man held the community together. Over eighty people had been killed in total and many of the children were orphans: some of them lived in the school. Gabriel told us that he had a problem getting the money together to feed them but they didn't want to be farmed out to relatives because they loved school so much. Right then I determined I'd find a way to make sure this man had the money to feed them. It was a promise I made to myself and I wouldn't forget it when I got back to London.

We spoke to a boy of about fourteen who'd been working when the gunmen burst in and started firing indiscriminately. Dropping behind the desk he hid for three terrifying hours.

Another lad rolled up his trouser leg to reveal a hideous scar on his shin. Flesh was missing to the bone, the scarring white and puckered so that it looked as if the leg had exploded from within. In a way it had: this was the exit wound for a bullet that hit behind his knee. After he was downed one of the raiders speared him. We saw a tiny girl with machete scars on her forearms; she couldn't have been more than three when it happened, her brother cut down right in front of her.

Gabriel took us to the mass graves; eighty-two villagers dead and twenty-two of them children. The marauders stole cattle, goats and donkeys, leaving the survivors with nothing. The graves were marked with beds of dry reeds and on the beds were personal belongings of those who'd been slaughtered. A small wooden barrel, a tin mug painted with flowers.

Little children killed with machetes; I found it very, very difficult.

COLOURS OF KENYA

We headed towards the lodge now; the road was a nightmare, shaking the bike to bits. My hands and feet were numb.

'Charley,' I said over the radio. 'Let's stop for a moment.'

We took a breather. 'Such incredible scenery,' Charley waved a hand at the vista, 'but you daren't look at it in case something goes bang.' He grinned. He was in his element. 'Mind you, I really like this kind of road, you have to concentrate so hard yet stay loose at the same time: it's really challenging.'

'Yeah, challenging, right. I like it about as much as I like sticking a needle in my eye.' I scanned the horizon. 'Look over there, Charley. That's either giraffe very far away or goats very near.'

We came to the turning finally; the track that led to the Marsabit Lodge, and it was probably as bad as anything we'd ridden so far. But oh boy, was it worth it. A 1950s-style lodge with log walls and a tin roof and a wide porch.

Beyond the buildings against the trees was the most magnificent waterhole. Clouds massed overhead, great wreaths of them reflected in the water. Banks of grasslands carried the slope, and beyond the lake these great swathes of trees. I stopped the bike and the smile just got wider. They were wandering amid the shallows. Oh my god. I'd ridden my bike to the elephants.

There was a family of them in the shallows on the far side of the waterhole. A squabble broke out among the youngsters and the adults came in, mum and dad, we could hear their bellows echo across the landscape.

When it got dark, the elephants wandered around the lake and came right up to the restaurant. We crawled on our stomachs to get closer without spooking them. That hundred and fifty miles of shit road had been worth every jar of the teeth, every curse. This was Africa, and I was lying in the grass with wild elephants a couple of yards away.

I could have stayed for days. There wasn't time, of course, and first thing in the morning we were on the road again, the really grim stuff now; big rocks and heavy dirt that kept the front wheel wobbling. I carried on, standing tall and keeping relaxed, thinking about the village ahead where we hoped to meet the Samburu people.

CHARLEY: We were into the red dirt again; cutting across the north-western corner of Kenya, heading towards the Losai National Park. We passed old and bent women carrying huge bundles of wood. The sights were different and yet similar to what we'd seen in

Ethiopia and it amazed me to see what these people had to do every day of their lives.

Claudio came off right in front of me, he was there one minute, down the next and I almost hit him. As it was, I had to lay my bike down. Classic case of riding too close when I spent my life reminding the other guys that we mustn't do that.

Clouds was really pissed off: 'Really,' he said, 'I don't like this sand. I hate it. Fucking hell, I never know what to do.'

'Just keep the power on,' I told him.

'I did that.' He gesticulated at the massive rut where he'd fallen.

'The wheel got caught in there, Clouds,' I told him. 'Locked the front and when you tried to power on it flipped you off.'

He went down again shortly afterwards. The sand was deep now: fesh fesh, like red talcum powder, so loose it was almost like riding on liquid.

We hit better roads finally. Open savannah, rolling hills in the distance and acacia trees offering a little shade.

The Samburu village was temporary. We met the chief, a man wearing the traditional red robes of his people, a sash over one shoulder similar in style to the Masai. It was hard to age him – late forties, early fifties perhaps – people out here have a hard life so he could have been a lot younger. He told us that the tribe had come together from various villages for a special ceremony; they were in the process of putting up their huts, made from a dome-shaped framework of poles covered by animal skins.

We asked the chief what the ceremony was and he told us that seventy young men were going to be circumcised. There was no anaesthetic and the boys must show no emotion, no twitch of an eye or curl of a toe whatsoever. The chief explained how the foreskin is cut in four places then peeled . . . well anyway, it sounded about as painful as it gets. He told us, with no hint of amusement, that his son was in the ceremony and if he so much as made a sound he'd kill him. Even now we don't know if he was joking.

We asked him if it would be possible to camp with them. He left us, and, gathering the elders, wandered over to the animal corral and discussed it. After a while he came back and said we could camp, only not in the village. He indicated an area about a hundred yards off. He asked us if we had a doctor with us. As part of the deal he wanted Dai to take a look at his wife: she'd given birth yesterday.

The village was buzzing with children, camels, donkeys, the bleating of young goats. Naked children were running around, little tots with shaved heads. The women wore the same red shawls as the men and many of them had weighted earrings that stretched the skin of their ear lobes. Both the men and women wore masses of brightly coloured necklaces and looked much like the Masai we'd seen near Kilimanjaro. We found out the two peoples were related and, as with the Masai, livestock was the Samburu livelihood. They were semi-nomadic and they kept cattle, donkeys, camels and goats. Their main food was milk: sometimes they mixed it with blood.

...OFF ROAD

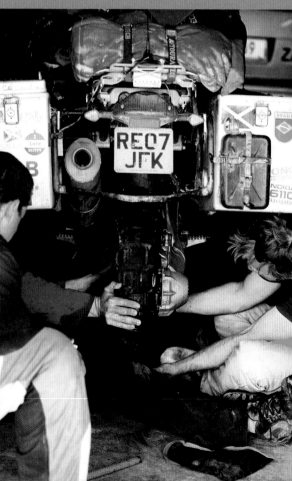

EWAN: Dai came out of the chief's tent and told us his wife would be fine. She was quite young, had bled heavily during the birth and had been suffering some stomach pains because of it. But he'd asked the other women if this was normal for her and having watched her give birth to three other children, they said it was. The placenta was out and the uterus retracted so nothing major was wrong. Dai gave her multi-vitamins, some iron tablets and paracetamol for the pain.

She was the chief's second wife, and he had six other children with his first one. Sitting in his other tent he told us he was thinking of getting a third wife and Charley piped up that Olly would beat him if he asked her even for a second wife.

The hut wasn't quite completed yet and the chief's first wife told us that it took about four days from start to finish. We sat on mats made from woven reeds and I was in my element; elephants last night and now the people. This was the Africa I'd dreamt we'd get to see. Young warriors, very cool, carrying sticks and spears. Hundreds of kids running around, everyone wanting to talk to us: it was marvellous.

I wandered among the livestock; donkeys who were tethered by their nostrils. At night all the animals were secured inside thorn bush corrals to stop hyenas or lions getting at them. The people seemed pretty well fed considering their diet of milk and blood; apparently they only ate meat on special occasions such as rites of passage ceremonies like circumcision. It made my eyes water just to think about it.

I watched the sun go down and exchanged a glance with Charley.

'Just another fucking perfect African sunset, Charley.'

That was our line, like Sarah Miles all bitter and twisted in *White Mischief*.

In the morning we said our goodbyes and hit the road once more.

Heading towards the equator the road was very dusty, and just when I thought I really was enjoying myself we hit more deep sand. This was worse than anything we'd seen – you could stir it, it was that soft. The bikes were all over the place; even Charley was finding it hard to cope. Great red clouds kicked up and in three miles we had ten separate incidents. I saw Claudio go down and my front end shook, the handlebars almost wrenched from my grasp.

'I don't like sand, Ewan,' Clouds was saying. 'No matter what Charley says, nothing works. Nothing works when you're riding in sand.'

Tell me about it, I thought.

A few yards further and he was off again. I was off. Then Claudio fell again. Jesus! Finally we hit the scrub and it was a joy to see hard gravel, big stones; feel the sudden jarring of washboard. I thought I hated the gravel, but that fesh fesh: it was worse than anything we'd encountered in Sudan.

We rode for a few miles on washboard and then the real drama began. Mud – no, not mud. A river crossing: actually it wasn't a river so much as a swamp. The road petered into nothing but brush and bushes with thorns that would impale you. There was a river

The conditions in Kenya were really challenging.

blocking our path. Not deep, but blood red and cushioned by great banks of mud that had water courses of their own, ponds, swampy little lakes. It was hard to see where the narrowest point was.

This was really challenging. At first I couldn't see a way through and Charley and I wandered indistinguishable paths trying to figure out a way across.

The trucks arrived and even our fixer seemed perturbed.

We took a walk, leaving the four-wheelers to consider their options while we tried to find a simpler way. We found a handsome young kid with a spear over his shoulder, chewing a stick; he was tending his cattle. We asked him about suitable spots and he pointed us off to the right.

On investigation it was about as good as we'd seen. The water was shallow; the mud not too deep. Prodding around with sticks we figured that with help, we could get the bikes over.

'We should move one of the trucks first,' Russ suggested, 'and that way we can thread the winch round the forks and drag the bikes over.'

Charley disagreed. 'Let the bikes go first,' he said. 'We'll walk them over. If the trucks go they'll churn up the bottom and we'll never get across.'

It was agreed. Charley and I played stone, paper, scissors and he won. With him guiding the throttle and clutch, me and two of the soldiers assisting, we wheeled his bike across the ruts into the soft stuff. We half drove, half pushed it through the water and up the far bank. We celebrated with much yelling and whooping.

With Charley's bike safe with the savannah stretching ahead, we went back for my bike and finally Claudio's. Then the trucks. The fixer tried to get his across first and it got well and truly stuck, listing badly in the mud, dirty brown water up to the door.

They decided to get our two trucks across and worry about the fixer's afterwards: drive hard and fast and get as far as they could, then fix the winch line to a fairly inadequate looking tree and haul the last bit.

Russ went first, really gunning the engine with Jim Foster knee deep in water alongside. He got a good distance but grounded in the mushy stuff and Jim attached the winch to the tree.

We hauled the truck out, then it was David's turn. He took a massive run up and steamed into the water. He got to the far bank and half up it before the wheels dug in. Winch attached he was out and half an hour later so was the fixer. We were covered in mud and grime, water and slime, but it was high fives and lots of whooping as we realised we'd overcome the most difficult natural challenge on the trip thus far.

CHARLEY: We were still full of it fourteen miles later when Claudio's shock absorber went again. I couldn't believe it – two BMW shocks and both had blown their oil seals. Professionals now, Ewan and I had it changed in ten minutes: even Claudio was impressed.

A few miles later the shock went again. Two in one day, three in two days: it was uncanny.

We fixed it again and I was thanking God for Addis and the chance we'd had to regroup. We hadn't had to replace a single shock absorber on Long Way Round and here we were with three in two days: five so far in total.

I loved it all, though: perhaps the hardest day, certainly the most challenging, and yet for me maybe the most rewarding. No matter what the road had thrown at us, we'd dealt with it.

Ewan pulled over, yelling at me across the radio. They'd been fixed in Addis Ababa. 'Charley, zebras; wild zebras.' He slapped his tank. 'My brothers and sisters. Look.'

There was a small herd by the side of the road that paused to take a look at us.

'I had no idea they were so big,' Ewan said.

'I don't remember their ears being that long, either.'

He laughed. 'Maybe they're the long-eared kind.'

The following morning we met Lola. You're wondering, maybe some Kenyan goddess, olive skinned and . . .

We took time out at a wildlife park and from the back of a jeep saw eland, impala, giraffe and white rhino. This was open country covered in green thorn bushes and yellow grass where I imagined lion or leopard lurking. Acacia trees offered a hint of shade and rocks jutted in massive distant cliffs. There was one enormous rhino, I mean huge, about thirty feet from the truck and Ewan was gobsmacked. 'I can't believe how long his horn is,' he said. 'I've only seen those stumpy little nubs but that's a huge long one.'

'Massive,' I echoed.

And there she was, square-faced with not even so much as a little nub of a horn. Lola the baby black rhinoceros being fed by a ranger from a two litre bottle. She was the sweetest thing you've ever seen, sucking away, long lashes across her eyes, skin all wrinkly and tough like an elephant.

She was fifty-six days old and her mother was blind and couldn't look after her. The same mother had had five other calves and hadn't been able to look after any of them either. It didn't seem to stop her hanging out with the guy rhinos, though.

Ewan quickly fell for the lovely baby black rhino, Lola – but sadly there was no more room on the back of his bike.

There were two rangers taking care of Lola twenty-four hours a day. They fed her a bottle of milk every three hours. The guy we spoke to rolled out a blanket at night and slept with her. He would be by her side for the next three to seven years until she decided she didn't need him any more and wandered into the bush.

Ewan and I took turns to feed her and she sucked noisily until all the milk was gone. After that she'd get really frisky and even though she was little she could knock you down. I took the odd whack and I tried to imagine being charged by an adult – you'd be in pieces.

The guide told us that the rhino population was increasing. There had been some really bad poaching about ten years ago, but the park held a hundred rhinos now and forty-eight of those were the endangered black variety. After her food and a bit of a play Lola crashed out – she lay on her side flicking her tail in the dust while Ewan stroked her chin.

'No, mate,' I said, catching the look in his eye. 'We've already earmarked a donkey sanctuary. I don't think even Eve would stand for a rhino.'

We were on tarmac when we made it to the equator. With everything that had happened I'd forgotten it was in Kenya that we'd cross to the southern hemisphere.

Staying the night at a small hotel in Nkuru I realised we were only half an hour from some friends, Rod and Claire Jones; they own a beautiful place on the shores of Lake Naivasha: I couldn't ride past their door without popping in for a cup of tea.

EWAN: It was an amazing place and gave us a taste of another kind of Africa. Claire's family had been in Kenya for generations and their lodge was exquisite. This was a hint of colonial Africa; a wide veranda and savage skies, the lake at the bottom of the garden. Claire keeps a small plane and she treated us to the most spectacular fly-past. We were in the air more than an hour and didn't once climb above seventy feet. Skimming across the wave tops, we saw hippo sleeping in the shallows, water buffalo, white-headed eagles skating the surface for fish. Everywhere the world was green, water plentiful – very different from the drier region we had just passed through.

We'd only meant to stop for breakfast but Rod and Claire persuaded us to stay the night. We took drinks and some food down to the shore for what they call a 'sundowner'. I could see a hippo in silhouette, the most dangerous animal in Africa. The sun was sinking, the night was cool, and the hippo slipped beneath the surface of the water.

It was our last night – the Kenyan adventure was over and we'd barely a month left on the road. At five the following morning we left for the Ugandan border.

WILD AT HEART

' I was profoundly shocked. Of course I had heard there were child soldiers in Uganda but I had no idea these massive Internally Displaced People's camps existed, no idea that young girls like Sarah had been so physically and psychologically ravaged. ' EWAN

17

UGANDA

SIZE DOES MATTER

PARIS

MONTREAL
NEW YORK
LIMA 13100
SA...AGO 12300
BRASILIA 9800
ANTANANARIVE 2700

SINGAPORE 8100 Km
TEHRAN 4500 Km
MOSCOW 7300 Km

CAIRO 4200 Km
BANGKOK 7300

NEW DELHI

STANBUL 5400 K
LAGOS 4000 K
KAMPALA
KINSHASA 2700
KINGSTON 9800
CAPETOWN 4700
LUSAKA 2500 K
UNIVERSITY 32

Don't try this at home.

EWAN: In a way, Uganda reminded me of Britain. It was very green, with rolling hills and grassy verges, and trees that somehow didn't look African. The people at the border were particularly friendly, going out of their way to wish us luck on the road. It was a wonderful introduction. The country felt pretty laid back and gentle, we were gliding along on good tarmac and I was really enjoying the riding.

We stopped at a coffee-sorting house owned by a consortium of over three thousand farmers who supplied Cafédirect with organic beans. I love coffee, and it had been one of the little unexpected pleasures on this trip. In Ethiopia they crush the beans then boil them over a charcoal burner. Then they pour it out and pour it back over and over again. By the time it's served black with a little sugar, it's wonderfully rich in flavour.

At the coffee-sorting house, we were greeted with the same enthusiasm and affection we'd experienced everywhere on this trip. The women wore bright clothes and head scarves, orange and purple, lime green. The manager greeted us; a tall man, well-built; he introduced us to the head of security who was even taller and more well-built.

Three thousand independent coffee growers – some of whom had five hundred plants, some as few as twenty; it didn't matter. They grew their coffee organically and brought the beans here. As a consortium they had the power to sell in quantity and cut out the middlemen. Good beans fetch a good price and this way the growers didn't lose out.

CHARLEY: The following morning we were on the road to Kampala and looking forward to our second UNICEF visit. We flew north from Kampala, despite the ceasefire, it was too dangerous to ride because of banditry and guerrilla incursion. There had been fighting in northern Uganda for twenty years between the Ugandan government forces (UPDF) and the Lord's Resistance Army (LRA) led by Joseph Kony.

Kony comes from the Gulu region and calls himself a spirit medium. When he was young he was a millennial fighter recruited by Alice Auma who led a rebellion in the mid-1980s after allegedly receiving visions from the Holy Spirit. Kony went his own way, however, and tried to fulfil his ambition of a state based on the Ten Commandments. His interpretation of the commandments seems a little vague, mind you; we were told that one of his edicts stated that you couldn't ride a bicycle and anyone who did had their legs chopped off.

The United States has proclaimed the LRA a terrorist organisation and in 2005 the International Criminal Court indicted Kony in his absence for crimes against humanity. The ceasefire was brokered by the government of Southern Sudan in 2006 and signed by both the LRA and UPDF.

Politics aside, children are the first victims in any war, and in northern Uganda their fate was particularly grim. Over a twenty-year period twenty-five thousand children were snatched from their homes. Families, villages, whole communities were destroyed. Afraid of constant attack, those who weren't snatched or murdered fled their homes and now one million four hundred thousand live in Internally Displaced People's camps.

The camp at Amuru seems to go on forever – thousands of little round huts with thatched roofs eating into the grasslands, built so close together their roofs all but interlock, creating a labyrinth of passageways between them. Forty-five thousand people living far too close to their neighbours, with no privacy, little sanitation and inadequate healthcare.

EWAN: We'd come to see Sarah and were invited to the hut she shares with her uncle and nine-month-old son, who was carried in a pouch on her back. Sarah is seventeen and was abducted by the LRA ten years ago. Quietly she told us what had happened to her. She has virtually no memories of life before the war. All she can recall is that she had two sisters who died, and she has two brothers who also live in the camp. Her eldest brother was killed in the fighting.

We had an amazing day meeting school children with UNICEF in Gulu Amuru.
Some were former child soldiers, and their stories affected us very deeply.

The LRA came to the village and took Sarah, her brother and lots of other children to train as new recruits: child soldiers. Aged just seven, she had to walk all the way to the border with Sudan, which can take four days by car. It was a forced march, the children not allowed to slow down, and if they did they were punished. Sarah got an infection in her foot and by the time they got to Sudan she was crawling, traumatised, bewildered and forced along by her captors on hands and knees.

After a brief period of rest she was forced into military training: guerrilla warfare, guns, mortars, machetes, hand-to-hand combat; unless they were pregnant or had a child the girls were treated exactly the same as the boys. Sarah was taught how to raid a village, how to maim, and how to kill. I repeat: she was seven years old.

The kids were brainwashed. Kony himself came to see new recruits, persuading them he'd rescued them from awful lives in remote villages where there was no hope of anything. He was a powerful and charismatic leader and lots of kids were sucked in. But not Sarah; she just wanted to go home. She didn't dare try to escape though – one girl who did was brought back and the new recruits were forced to beat her to death.

Watching her die, Sarah vowed she'd never try to escape. She'd take whatever was thrown at her and somehow she'd survive.

She was given to a local commander as a wife and maltreated by his other wives, older women, who starved and beat her. When she was twelve she heard her brother had been killed and she became very, very depressed. She cried for days, refused to eat; she became so desperate that she decided she'd try to flee.

She was shot during her escape attempt and brought back.

Having been beaten, she became pregnant in 2005. Unable to keep up when the camp moved, Sarah was released by her commander and after walking for days she arrived at a UPDF camp. From there she was moved to a UNICEF-supported World Vision reception centre where she received counselling and her parents were traced.

At first she suffered terribly – flashbacks, nightmares about killing and combat; what she'd seen, what she'd been forced to do. Gradually, however, the flashbacks dwindled and the nightmares became less frequent. When she was finally reunited with her parents she was so shocked she couldn't talk. She had to tell them her brother had been killed and discovered that they'd heard rumours and had already held a funeral for him; even though at that time, unknown to them, he was still alive.

These days Sarah lives with her uncle because although her family accepted her back, her father died shortly afterwards and her mother has only a little piece of ground to grow food and is also looking after orphans. Sarah has missed out on her schooling – she hasn't been in class since she was seven and with a baby at seventeen it's too late.

She's learned to use a sewing machine and has a tiny tailoring business in the square. Her life is very tough but she's happier than she was, and she's part of a group supported by UNICEF called 'Empowering Hands'. Sarah helps other displaced and abducted children, 'come back home kids' as they're derogatorily called, to reintegrate into society.

There's a lot of suspicion and fear amongst the people because many who weren't abducted believe the ones that were went to the LRA voluntarily. People like Sarah raided villages, killing, maiming and abducting other children. There's huge distrust. When she first arrived at Amuru she was too scared to go outside.

I was profoundly shocked. Of course I had heard there were child soldiers in Uganda but I had no idea these massive Internally Displaced People's camps existed, no idea that young girls like Sarah had been so physically and psychologically ravaged.

Charley and I left her hut in silence; neither of us quite knowing what to say, aware that we'd been in the presence of a dignified young woman who was desperately trying to come to terms with what had happened and to pick up the pieces of her life.

We then went to St Martin's school in the neighbouring Copee camp where the children wore white shirts and maroon shorts and gave us a wonderful welcome. We'd come to deliver supplies from UNICEF – what they call 'school in a box' – which is one of the many really positive things happening in northern Uganda.

One thing I see over and over again in Africa is the passion the kids have for school. They hunger for it, so conscious that education is the only way they can have any kind of future. That's why 'school in a box' is such a great idea: a box containing all the materials to set up a classroom for eighty children – pens, little blackboards, chalk and notebooks. Each box costs £120 and Charley and I delivered ten to St Martin's. We handed out the goodies to each child; a UNICEF bag containing two jotters, a couple of pencils, a ruler and a pencil sharpener. The kids were all scrumming round us, desperate not to miss out.

 The box didn't just contain school books, but skipping ropes and footballs too; we watched the absolute delight a football gave them. No sooner was it out of the box than a game began that was about ninety-five a side.

CHARLEY: They called us 'Sir' which sounded strange but nice. They have a tough life, they really do, yet they're so hopeful; especially the young ones. It was a tragedy that Sarah and thousands like her had missed out. Daniel, however, still has a chance. He is being taught at the level of a twelve-year-old even though he is fifteen. But at least he is in school. We sat with him in his hut and he was wearing a football shirt, looking for all the world like any other teenager. Except for his eyes. His eyes were deep, very deep, and they looked way older than he did.

His village had been right in the path of one of the LRA's raiding routes. They would pass through abducting people, cutting them down with machetes. They didn't kill everyone, some they just disfigured; cutting off lips, ears, eyelids . . . and leaving their

victim alive. Daniel was abducted when he was seven and remained with the LRA until he was ten. He was one of hundreds in the camps. When the raiders came to Daniel's village he was given a choice: go with the LRA or be killed. He was terrified – it's so hard to imagine a child younger than both Doone and Kinvara being given that choice. Come with us or die, the soldiers told him. It was no choice at all.

And the parents, I couldn't begin to imagine what they must have gone through. Their sons and daughters abducted; never knowing if they were alive or dead, if they'd been raped, beaten, maimed.

Daniel saw people killed and their bodies dumped in streams he'd have to drink from. Bloodied streams; he was drinking the blood of his so-called enemies. He was taught to use a machine gun, a machete, mortars; he was taught to raid villages and strike fear into people. He was taught how to kill. He saw people killed and he wasn't even ten years old.

He managed to escape during a firefight with the Ugandan government forces; his unit was scattered and together with an older boy he just ran and kept on running. After being gone three years, somehow Daniel was able to find his way back to his home town. But infected with the fear of re-abduction he went to Gulu town to stay with an aunt. He got involved with Empowering Hands and countered any stigma he felt about being a 'come back home kid'.

The visit ended on a high: we helped UNICEF doctors with a programme of inoculation – little vials of polio vaccine for the children, jabs for their mothers, de-worming tablets. The camps are vast and poor; the sanitation and healthcare limited, and all the schools are overcrowded.

The people gathered for us yet again and we sang, played drums and danced. They love to dance in Africa. The drums were amazing, that heavy 'jungle beat' really gets into your soul. One poignant image will stick in my mind, though, of a tiny, malnourished kid, stomach distended under a raggedy green jumper. He was holding a toy pistol.

Leaving the camps, heading on towards the border with Rwanda, I had one thought in my mind. The things that will free these children are health and education.

'Suddenly we saw movement in the trees, a smudge of black; a couple of young gorillas playing high in the branches. I couldn't believe it; they were about twenty metres away. ' CHARLEY

18

RWANDA

ANOTHER COUNTRY

EWAN: Certain countries create certain impressions before you actually get to them: sometimes those impressions prove to be correct and sometimes they don't. Rwanda is a prime example of one that didn't. Thirteen years ago the country was in the grip of civil war. One million people were massacred in one hundred days while the West pretty much ignored what was happening. Bill Clinton said that not doing anything to help was one of his biggest regrets during his eight years as US president.

We were at the border in plenty of time to meet up with our fixer; our plan being to get to a lodge close to the Virunga Mountains before we stopped for the night. It took an hour of waiting before we realised we were at the wrong border.

The fixer was at another crossing eighty miles to the south.

Finding the place on the map, Charley and I set off into the mountains. As we hit the twisty stuff the good tarmac suddenly gave way to dirt. We were climbing, the road switching back on itself, and the riding was much tougher than either of us had expected. These eighty miles were going to take longer than we anticipated. Heading into a narrow pass, we saw a line of trucks backed up, and a little further discovered that an articulated lorry had overturned and was blocking the road both ways. It had clearly been there a while because the spilled cargo was being loaded into other trucks.

There was no way Russ and David would get through so Charley got on the phone and told them they would have to find an alternative route. The overturned truck had left the slimmest of gaps however, and we nosed the bikes between the cab and the grassy bank.

We thought the trucks would be miles behind and as they had the carnets we had no chance of crossing into Rwanda that night. But then Charley heard them talking over the radio and looking down we could see them on another stretch of road hundreds of metres below us. Their detour had been quicker than the original route. We got to the trucks, grabbed the carnets and sped off again. If we could get to the border before it closed we might persuade the Rwandans to wait for the others.

It was the strangest border crossing I've ever seen: a single dirt track edged by terraced hillsides with no vehicles save one bus and our bikes. People were walking, carrying great loads on their heads, there was the odd bicycle stacked with wood, but that was about it and I didn't really believe it was the right road until we actually got there. It was the crossing, though, no matter what it looked like, with a ragged looking bloke with no uniform operating the barrier.

The trucks made it and a couple of hours later we were again doing what we'd vowed we wouldn't – riding in Africa at night.

I felt quite emotional riding through a country with such a terrible history of unbelievable violence, but still so beautiful. Just a couple of miles in we stopped for a moment and were immediately surrounded by adults as well as children. As I looked at their faces all I could think of was what this nation had been through. I wondered how on earth it had managed to heal itself.

CHARLEY: We were going to Virunga to see the mountain gorillas made famous by Dian Fossey. We would have just an hour with them – more than that and any coughs, colds or infections we might be carrying could be transmitted to the animals. We stayed the night in the lodge and the next morning drove an hour and a half to a village at the edge of the rain forest. We were introduced to armed rangers who would guide us, then started out on foot. We were at eighteen hundred metres and the gorillas lived at three thousand metres. From the village we could see the mountains shrouded in a blue mist. There were lots of villages round here – it was farming country, coffee growers mostly, and one of the most densely populated areas of the country. The land was very green, the soil looked good and we walked a mud road laced with heavy stones and bordered by green hedges.

It was tough going and the air was thin and damp, though fortunately it wasn't raining. It was quite cold, though, and we were wearing waterproofs; once into the forest proper we'd be waist-high in foliage.

Our guide told us that poaching was still a problem, and with ongoing fighting in neighbouring Democratic Republic of Congo the gorillas on this side of the border had to be monitored carefully. He spoke English with a French accent – many people speak French in Rwanda because it was once a Belgian colony.

'Ewan speaks French,' I said. 'Exquisite French, don't you, Ewan?'

'Yes,' he said. 'It's a particular kind of French that's actually called "exquisite". Not fluent, just exquisite. I don't know many words, or French grammar or anything, but what I do know I can say very, very well. Not much use but nice to listen to.'

We climbed into the forest now, the villages far behind. We were following a narrow path that drifted through a sea of green and every now and again we'd come to a clearing and get another view of the mountains. Then suddenly we saw movement in the trees, a smudge of black; a couple of young gorillas playing high in the branches. I couldn't believe it; they were about twenty metres away.

As we came out of the trees there in front of us was a female lying on her side with three youngsters, including one new baby. Very quietly we sat down to watch them. As

we looked on the baby started suckling. It was amazing to be this close – the guide had explained that if we were lucky we might get within seven metres but they were no more than a metre away.

The guide showed us how to make grunting noises that indicated we meant no harm; he also said if we blew raspberries it would get their attention – both were noises that gorillas made themselves.

Then suddenly he told us to get up and move back.

A massive silverback was striding up the slope. He walked on his knuckles, belly hanging, massive shoulders; his head was absolutely huge. We moved up the hill to let him past and he ambled slowly by, looking sideways at us from about ten feet.

EWAN: They were all around us now. The mother got up and wandered off and behind us another silverback appeared. He was even bigger than the first one, sitting there chewing on a stalk; they eat the wild celery that grows here and that sticky grass you get in Britain that clings to your clothes. The food was everywhere in abundance; they just had to reach out and grab whatever they wanted. Another smaller gorilla sauntered by, long arms and short legs. Charley blew a raspberry and it stopped and studied us.

'She is beautiful,' Charley said. 'Amazing eyes, really beautiful. I think I'm falling in love.' He paused for a moment then added. 'Normally I prefer blondes but this one . . .'

'I think it's a young male, Charley.'

It was the most incredible hour and as we came down we saw another silverback, sitting on a mound so most of his body was visible above the foliage. He watched us, great head, huge shoulders, an air of nonchalance about him, and then he stood up and, like a king surveying his domain, gazed across the forest.

We were able to get unbelievably close to the gorillas in the Rwandan jungle.

Staff at the Bourbon Coffee Shop: a great example of Rwandans creating a better future for themselves and their country.

The minister of tourism had arranged the trip and we met her in the Bourbon Coffee Shop in Kigali later that day. She explained that tourism was an important way for Rwanda to establish a stable economy. In the past year thirteen thousand tourists from ninety-five different countries had visited Virunga, and 5 per cent of the revenue generated by the gorillas was reinvested among the village communities of the area. She explained that since the war ended the people were only looking forward: the whole country was determined to move on. It was all about moving forward; the genocide of 1994 was part of Rwanda's history, it wasn't going to decide the future.

We chatted to the owner of the Bourbon Coffee Shop, a very cool guy who served great coffee. He said that since the genocide, people would say they were no longer Hutu or Tutsi, they were simply Rwandan. He'd quit the corporate life he'd been living to open his cafe and now he dealt directly with the coffee growers, most of whom had had no idea of the value of their product or indeed had ever tasted a cup.

The place was vibrant, heaving with people; NGOs, doctors, nurses, aid workers and volunteers. We spoke to a couple of American girls who told us that at the end of every month there was a day of public works where the people would do something for their country. For such a historically divided nation there was an overwhelming feeling of unity.

Before we left, the minister of tourism invited us to her brother's wedding reception that evening. We didn't really have the right clothes, but turned up (rather underdressed), got past security and met the president (as you do), Paul Kagame, who had raised an army in Uganda and overthrown the Hutu militia. Half an hour later the minister found us again and told us that the president had asked us to his country house at eleven the following morning.

Over dinner there was a note of caution. Charley pointed out that we knew nothing about this man at all. We'd heard different rumours about his reputation – some good, some bad – but we decided in the end that we should go and at least try to make up our own minds.

I asked our fixer, Daddy, why the West hadn't got involved. He just shrugged and said that Rwanda was a small country and back in 1994 Nelson Mandela was being sworn in as president of South Africa. He reminded me that there had been war raging in the Balkans and a football world cup in the USA. He said that most people couldn't find Rwanda on a map and with so much else going on, no one was that bothered.

Canada had led a small peacekeeping force, but when they requested more troops and permission to intervene in the slaughter, the UN had turned them down. The French sent soldiers – not to stop the militia but to protect them from Paul Kagame's invaders.

An audience with the president. We'd already turned up at one function underdressed and didn't want to do so again. So we bought suits and shirts; the trousers too long and held up with gaffer tape. I found a pair of white pointed shoes that made me laugh. Suitably dressed we set off on the bikes for the Rwandan President's residence.

CHARLEY: The house was big but not too big, understated, maybe, compared to what you'd expect in Europe. It nestled among some trees like a big old ranch house, only made of brick. Inside we were shown to a meeting room with an absolutely enormous round table. An array of spears decorated one wall.

We stepped onto the veranda, the back of the house overlooking pastures where black cattle with gigantic horns were grazing. The president kept them for milk and later we tried some. It tasted like natural yoghurt and was delicious. Beyond the pastures there was a lake surrounded by hills; beyond that was the Tanzanian border – our next destination. It was very beautiful, tranquil, and it was only then I thought about how clean Rwanda felt and noticed that livestock were fenced off from the road. Though we saw plenty of people walking, some carrying huge loads on their heads, there were no donkeys, sheep or cattle on the streets.

The president arrived and we shook hands again. We discussed the challenges he had faced, and asked him what motivated him.

He explained that war was part of Rwandan history, both before independence from Belgium and certainly since. He and his family had fled to Uganda when he was three and he grew up in a refugee camp. He'd spent twenty-five years there and needed no motivation other than that. He formed the Rwandan Patriotic Front, raised an army and invaded. After he became president he asked the people a question: 'Why did we lose a million people in less than a hundred days?' He made them think about it, the everyday Rwandan.

The answer was bad politics, bad leadership and extremism.

Kagame said that he was determined not to see that repeated and pointed out that investment follows if a country can show it is both secure and stable.

Reminders of the horrors of the genocide in Rwanda were never far away. These bones are kept in the church at Natarama to remember the thousands that were butchered there.

Paul Kagame has many critics as well as supporters, and neither Ewan nor I could claim to be experts on Rwandan politics. But we both sensed, riding through Rwanda, that this is a country full of hope and optimism. The progress in thirteen years seems incredible. The Rwandans have succeeded where others maybe have failed – perhaps in part because they never forget what happened, and are so determined to make sure it never happens again. Genocide is part of their history but it isn't going to decide their future.

When this unexpected visit was over, we visited the Eglise Natarama, a Catholic church where five thousand people hid from the Hutu Interahamwe militia in 1994. They'd fled from villages and taken refuge in the old brick church with its concrete pews and dirt yard. The militia arrived and lobbed grenades through the windows. The ones who survived ran outside and were bludgeoned to death with hammers and machetes or decapitated with *pangas*. Others were herded into the outbuildings and burned alive: five thousand people in one day.

Their bones lie on shelves in the old church; thousands of skulls, some still impaled with spear shafts, others smashed where hammers hit them. From floor to ceiling, thousands and thousands of skulls. The clothes of the victims hang in a macabre collage, torn, burned, bloodstained. It was one of the most disturbing sights I've ever seen. It felt so at odds with the Bourbon Coffee Shop, the bustling streets, the sense of progress in the country.

Time and again we had seen the effects of war and brutality on this trip, just as we had ridden along the Road of Bones in Russia. We had spoken to mine victims in Ethiopia, child soldiers in Uganda. Now here again we were in a country that had been ripped apart by war; the genocide of a million civilians that, as Kagame said, had achieved absolutely nothing.

But in each of these countries we also found hope for the future.

I'd recommend anyone to visit Rwanda and if the people can go on rebuilding, continue to heal, then who knows, perhaps one day the bones at Natarama can be laid to rest.

' Crossing into Tanzania we were back on the great savannah; the world drier and dustier, yellow grass and grey dirt, a horizon marked only by the distant mountains. ' CHARLEY

19

TANZANIA

DESTINATION: 'TRANSIT'

CHARLEY: We'd allowed ourselves five days in Tanzania, but Eve was meeting us at the border with Malawi, and I knew Ewan would be itching to get there.

Once again, there was a huge change as we crossed the border. Rwanda was vibrant, very clean. Crossing into Tanzania we were back on the great savannah; the world drier and dustier, yellow grass and grey dirt, a horizon marked only by the distant mountains.

We got our heads down early and the following morning we were off at dawn. We stopped in a little town for lunch and Ewan took a phone call – Eve in Malawi.

His grin couldn't have got any wider.

EWAN: The following day the riding was much tougher, we were in really deep sand. Then with no warning the sand would be gravel, then rock, and you had no time to get used to it before it changed again.

Claudio went down, I went down . . . even Charley went down. I was getting tired again. I'd enjoyed the dirt yesterday but this was purgatory; really deep troughs and there was no way you could stand on the pegs, you just had to squat in the saddle, try and steer whilst paddling away at the ground with your feet. The front wheel would be bucking, the rear wheel snatching and losing traction in equal measure.

For lunch we ate cold boil-in-the-bag, which actually tasted better than it does hot. We had a kip and rode on and, after twelve hours of sand, rock and dirt we came to the camp.

Before we got to the camp, however, we hit the gnarliest piece of road we'd come across yet: a final two kilometres that felt like eighteen, a real kick in the balls. Troughs so deep they could've drawn water. If we thought we were paddling before, we were paddling now and by the time we finally got to the camp my legs felt as though someone had taken a piece of two-by-four and beaten them.

It was worth it, though. We pulled up as the sun was sinking and it really is that huge fireball you see in the movies. The savannah stretched out endless before us. A herd of elephants wandered towards the stream that cut the plain like a sliver of silver. This was the Katuma River; all there was until the rains came, at which time most of this grassland would become swamp.

The camp itself was fantastic; old school colonial with big tents, our own bathrooms where water-filled barrels created showers with strings to turn the water on and off. We had wooden beds with white linen and real pillows – oh, was I looking forward to hitting the hay tonight.

We were due a day off and in the morning we went in search of wildlife, sitting in the back of an open jeep. The Katavi National Park is part of the Serengeti and, unlike other parks, if we did see wildlife we were allowed to leave the jeep and walk. There were lions here and leopards, cheetahs, but we didn't see any. We did see elephants and a great herd of zebras, masses of them gathered at the river – and gigantic herds of Cape buffalo.

Russ and David and our whole team were behind us, on every step of our journey.

A warm welcome from some children as we travelled to the border with Malawi.

CHARLEY: The next day Ewan was up at some ungodly hour, packing his bike wearing a head torch – in less than forty-eight hours he would see his beloved wife.

We were away at dawn but before we'd properly left the camp I was down the road without my bike. I saw the tree stump. I watched the tree stump. Don't hit the stump, Charley, you can't hit the stump. I hit the stump and landed face down in the dirt.

Nothing broken, though, just another dent in the bike – and by early afternoon we were on hard dirt and doing seventy miles an hour. Ewan was on a mission now; we knew that Eve was already at the border and he couldn't wait to get there.

EWAN: Eve was so close and I was just dying to get to her. I was up at the crack of dawn, we were on the road by seven and it was four hours to the border. Finally, my heart hammering in my chest, there it was. A dirt road cutting through a gully with green hills rising in the distance – somewhere over there was my wife and I was so impatient to see her I cannot tell you.

20

MALAWI

LILONGWE DOWN

CHARLEY: I'd never seen Ewan quite so excited. As soon as the last of the paperwork was completed he raced across the border to Eve. I could understand it; if it had been Olly I'd have been jumping the fence.

I made my way through and there was Eve. Ewan leapt off the bike and she was in his arms. She looked terrific in her LWD hat and yellow singlet. He just held her and held her. In the end I had to look away. I mean, there was lots of kissing and hugging, lots . . .

It was great to see her and a relief she'd made it safe and sound. Rick, the last of our fixers, had freighted her bike from South Africa. He was driving a Nissan pickup that had been decked out with stickers like our trucks so it would be a unified front when we crossed the finish line in Cape Town.

Talking of stickers, Eve's bike was naked. Ewan quickly pasted a Long Way Down sticker onto the bike while I gave Eve a squeeze.

'How are you?'

'I just can't believe I'm here.'

She was, though, and Ewan was delighted. A little while later she was kitted out in a rally suit and crash helmet and was ready to go. She climbed on her bike, very nervous but determined to ride.

Ewan rode up alongside. 'OK, Eve?' he called.

'I'm so nervous,' she said.

'You'll be fine. Charley will go ahead and you follow him. I'll be right behind you.'

I swivelled round in the saddle. 'Now listen, Eve, no wheelies, all right?'

'Yeah,' Ewan echoed. 'Keep the front wheel on the ground.'

We set off at a gentle pace and I checked my mirrors. Eve was doing fine; she seemed relaxed and was riding smoothly. I watched her easing into the bends and getting a feel for the bike. I really admired her; it's gutsy what she was doing, not easy being dropped into Africa when you're inexperienced and getting on a bike with your husband and his mate who've been riding every day for months.

Eve was looking good, though.

EWAN: Once I'd got over the initial excitement, I couldn't quite believe Eve was here. I cast my mind back to that Sunday when she first said she wanted to go – remembering the delight and the worry. I recalled the arguments we'd had, the discussions with Charley, and yet here she was in front of me riding a 650 through Malawi. I was singing I was so happy.

Peeling off the highway we hit dirt road, heading for a remote lodge at the northern end of the lake. I was conscious that Eve only had half a day's off-road experience in her life. The dirt wasn't too bad to begin with, though, and she was cutting along beautifully. Then she dropped her bike right in front of me. My heart was in my mouth. But she got to her feet immediately, picked the bike up and was back in the saddle again.

I yelled out to see if she was OK. She was fine, she said, determined to carry on. Knowing Eve her pride was probably more bruised than anything. Back in the saddle she paddled the bike forward, trying to make it through the sand. Then she was down again and I had visions of myself back in Sudan.

We suggested to Eve that she ride in the truck for this last section, and David jumped on the bike. He was wearing a T-shirt with no helmet or gloves: he dropped the bike, grazed his elbow and got back on. We got a little further and he dropped it again.

Finally we made it to the lodge. David was fine, if a little bloody.

'Are you all right, mate?' I asked him.

'Now I know about sand. Jesus Christ, how the hell have you guys managed to cope with so much of it?'

'A case of having to, Dave,' I told him. 'You get used to it.'

'Not if your name's Claudio.' Clouds walked past me, shaking his head. 'Fucking sand, it's shit. Slow down, power on: it doesn't make any difference.'

Eve was tired and a bit shaky from picking the bike up but she told me the pain was worth it.

'The sand though, it's just much harder than it looks.'

The lodge was built above a small beach, with an open area of tables on a veranda, and the lake stretching blue and grey to the horizon. It was so beautiful, our bungalows overlooked the beach, a handful of trees, and water as far as the eye could see. Just about the perfect retreat for a man who hasn't seen his wife in a couple of months.

CHARLEY: The three of us rode together, the pace easy and Eve riding well. She kept it smooth and I was pleased for her because I wasn't sure how much she'd be able to do once we got to Zambia. The latest news was that there was some pretty serious off-roading ahead of us.

I loved Malawi. I've heard it called a 'hand-out-state', and it's true that UNICEF is active here, as is Christian Aid. But hand-outs or not, there's not much of an economy. The people were so friendly, they didn't hassle or crowd you and I hadn't once felt threatened. But then I'd felt that about every country we'd been through.

We were headed for a place called 'Cool Running', a campsite at the southerly end of the lake. Venturing down to the lake we had to leave the tarmac, and Eve found herself on dirt once again. She didn't fall through: feet out, she paddled the bike all the way down the slope.

At the camp site we met Steve and Dana. Steve was this crazy guy from Cape Town, and Dana was from Israel. They'd met at a trance party. Steve was a massive *Long Way Round* fan, and couldn't believe it when we showed up in the very spot where he was camping. He was living in a roof tent on top of a truck. He told us that he'd been so inspired by *Long Way Round* that he decided to follow a dream he'd always had. He sold everything: house, business, the lot. He bought the truck and the tent, hooked up with Dana and drove all over Africa. They'd landed here in Malawi and planned to start a lodge somewhere close to the lake.

I'd never met a more infectious soul or someone who laughed quite as much. He told us how much he admired what we'd done, but we were well known and didn't have to take on a challenge like Long Way Round; we could've stayed safe in our careers back in London.

'We're not that hardcore,' Ewan told him. 'I mean, there are plenty tougher than us. Remember Addis, Charley?'

I rolled my eyes: 'Oh God, yeah.'

Ewan explained. We were riding out of the city and had pulled up for a moment. This little kid walked over and in the strongest south London accent imaginable, he said: 'Where is you boys from, innit?'

'London,' I told him.

'London, is it. I'm from London. Whereabouts in London, innit?'

'Fulham,' Charley said.

'Fulham!' He looked aghast. 'You posh boy rough riders then, innit.'

EWAN: We set out again and Eve carefully negotiated the dirt from 'Cool Running' and as we hit tarmac she came alongside me.

'Did you see that, Ewan? Zambia will be like a tea party for me.'

We stopped early that day at another lodge near the capital Lilongwe. The rest of the team was there and Russ said he and David wanted to interview me for the website. We were sitting on a veranda and I was thinking how mellow it was meandering along with my wife.

Russ disappeared for a few moments and I was thinking, Where's he gone now? I thought we were doing an interview. He came back again and said he'd ordered a coke for me, which of course was very thoughtful.

He had the biggest smile on his face. He glanced at David.

'What . . . ?' I looked from one to the other, both grinning like a pair of prize Cheshire cats.

'Here's your coke,' Dave said.

I looked round and the waitress handed me the coke. 'Thanks,' I said then jumped, and I mean physically. The waitress looked just like – the waitress was my mum. I did a double take. The last time I'd spoken to Mum she'd been at home in Crieff and now here she was in the flesh handing me a can of coke.

'Hello,' I said. 'What're you doing here?'

She gave me a big hug and told me she'd come out to make sure I was behaving myself.

The reception we got at a UNICEF project in Malawi was fantastic and we felt privileged to be part of it all.

It was fantastic, a real surprise, just about the last thing I would've expected. She told me Russ had brought her out and suggested she could kill two birds with one stone by looking in on Sightsavers, a charity she's involved with here in Malawi.

'He suggested it to me at the premiere of *Miss Potter*,' Mum said, sitting down.

'*Miss Potter*!' I couldn't believe it. 'That was a year ago.'

'Planning ahead, mate,' Russ said with a smile. 'Dave and I thought it would be nice, you know, given Eve would probably be here too.'

I was gobsmacked. I really didn't know what to say: typical Russ and Dave, thinking about a gesture like this as far back as a year ago.

It was wonderful to see my mum, but all too quickly our time in Malawi was coming to an end. Hooking up with Sarah and Wendy from UNICEF, we set off for a community childcare centre in Chimteka to see how under-fives whose lives had been affected by HIV were being assisted.

UNICEF supports thousands of these centres all through Africa – they're usually set up in or close to villages and the young kids go there in the morning. They get food and some basic education, they play with their mates and are able to just be kids for a while. This time out also gives whoever is caring for them a chance to earn some money.

One in every thirteen people in Malawi is HIV positive and over half a million children have lost either one or both parents to an AIDS-related illness. The communities struggle to cope with the enormous amount of orphans left behind, and centres like this give them a chance to keep going.

CHARLEY: The young kids were amazing, racing around like any other children, laughing, shouting, playing. We received a fantastic welcome of songs and dancing. We had lunch of maize, beans and cabbage. The children were so happy to be around us, full of mischief and laughter. It always staggers me how positive even the youngest of them are.

After lunch we sat down with some of the older kids. Fausita, a thirteen-year-old girl, lost her parents when she was six. Since then she has lived across the road from the centre with her aunt. Fausita told us she loved coming to the centre because she had a lot of support from the people there, both the helpers and the other kids. She wanted to be a doctor when she grew up. The only problem is that secondary education in Malawi costs money and she has no parents to fund her.

Fausita is a good student, though, and she works very hard. UNICEF told us that because of that she has a good chance at secondary education and there are bursaries available with only a small contribution necessary from the child.

Malawi is such a small country, and it's all too easy for it to be forgotten. There's only one doctor for every 100,000 people and UNICEF, along with other non-government agencies, is doing all it can. Because the spread of HIV is so rife, extended families take on thousands of orphaned children. Fausita's aunt, for example, has seven to care for in all.

Often it's the grandmother, and we met a lady called Haviloina who couldn't tell us how old she was, she only knew her husband had been born in 1938. She thought she was around seventy, maybe, and had seen three of her six children die from what she called coughs and swelling. She had four grandchildren that she was now effectively mother to, and two of them were under five years old. It was such a lot for an older woman to take on, and yet she accepted her situation with grace and courage.

This was our final UNICEF visit and we said our goodbyes, thanking everyone for their hospitality, and thanking UNICEF for the care they continue to bring to these remote and potentially forgotten corners of the world. It's a privilege and a responsibility to make sure we keep their profile high because the people that read our books and watch the TV shows have been superb in supporting our charities financially. It's not just UNICEF, but CHAS of course and Riders for Health.

While we were in Kenya, the Day of Champions auction was held at the British Moto GP at Donnington Park. Every year the proceeds go to Riders for Health and, as we were watching elephants at a waterhole, we took a phone call and were told that two guys had paid a combined total of £22,000 to fly out and ride with us into Cape Town. It was an amazing gesture and, given that we found out while we were watching some incredible African wildlife, I think it really brought the trip home for both of us.

We were approaching the southern tip of Africa and I realised that it wasn't just Ewan and I travelling; we had every fan, every reader, every biker who followed our trail, all on the back of the bikes with us.

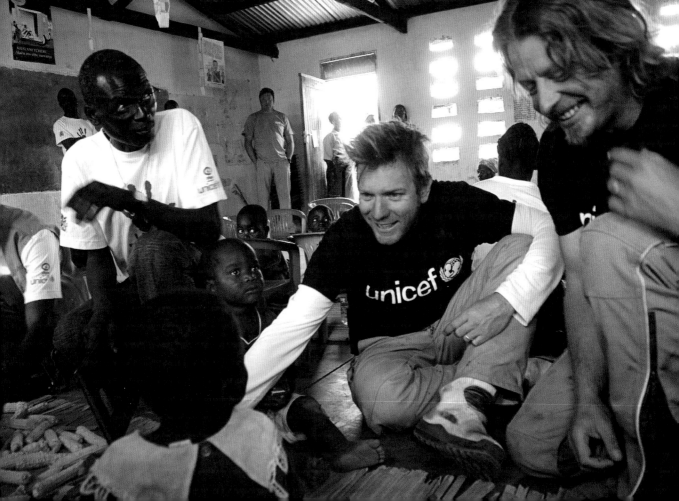

21

ZAMBIA

OUT IN THE CUDS
WITH THE GIRLS

EWAN: Eve rode with us for seven days and her riding got better and better. The time passed far too quickly though, each morning I'd wake with her beside me and think about the day ahead of us and then in no time it seemed to be evening again.

In Zambia the roads were actually much easier than we'd thought and Eve was hammering along at seventy, smooth as silk and dancing around the potholes like a veteran. We were heading for Victoria Falls where Charley planned to throw himself off a bridge with a bit of elastic tied round his feet.

Good luck, mate. I couldn't imagine doing it. Strangely, I'm not into anything where I think I might die.

We bumped into another biker, a guy from South Africa who'd zigzagged his way through Namibia and was heading for Malawi before drifting south again through Mozambique. Like us he was loaded to the gunwales. It was good to chat to him; we'd met plenty of cyclists en route but few bikers. He told us he worked in China and once his trip was over he was headed for Beijing and a language course in Mandarin.

On our travels we had heard about an old guy from Scotland called Ian McGregor Bruce who ran a crocodile farm. He sounded like a cross between Robert Shaw's character

On the road with Eve. We were amazed how good she was. She had only been riding for six months!

At the crocodile farm, with owner Ian McGregor Bruce – a fantastic character, with some interesting scars.

in *Jaws* and Crocodile Dundee. So we decided to drop in. When we arrived at the farm, he was at their educational centre in Livingstone, so we were greeted by his son.

They'd started the place twenty years ago when Ian was sixty. At eighty, he still played beach volleyball every day. His son told us he'd been a big game hunter and used to wrestle crocs. Gaining something of a reputation, he was called in by villagers to deal with problem crocs, big bastards that ate cattle and people. He started to catch them and bred them to provide skins for the leather industry. One thing led to another, and realising the tourist potential, they opened the educational centre in Livingstone.

Ian's son showed us one massive beast lying beside his pond, as big as a horse. He must have been twelve feet long. They'd caught him after he ate a couple of cows, followed by the men who owned them. When they brought him in there was one other male croc on the farm. This new guy was eighty years old already and he took on the other male, bit him in half and stole his nineteen wives.

Later we met Ian himself and he was exactly as I imagined. He had a broad Scots accent even after spending most of his life in Africa; he wore a green cap and wandered around with a long spiked pole. In one enclosure he messed about with a hissing, albino crocodile that moved so fast it was frightening.

'She's out of her element,' he told us, 'vulnerable on land.'

Vulnerable! She looked about as vulnerable as a tank.

CHARLEY: Ian reminded me of my dad, a slightly smaller version maybe, but just as sharp and funny. He introduced us to Maramba, another maneater who was even bigger than the cattle killer. He was lying in the mud with Peggy, so named because her right hind leg had been bitten off. Ian explained that even in the most filthy, rancid water a croc's wound never becomes infected. He told us that at two hundred million years old this reptile was about as evolved as it got and its stomach could digest pretty much anything.

We had just enough time to hear some grisly stories of Ian's hunting days, and see his collection of loaded rifles, before we had to head off. I had an appointment to keep with that length of elastic.

Before we left he told us to remember when we were camping in the bush that the leopard is the most treacherous animal in Africa. If you wound one, he will play dead and wait for you. When you get to him he'll pounce. A leopard did that to him once, ripped his cheek with a forepaw, nearly got his jugular and only narrowly missed ripping his stomach open with its hind legs.

Ewan was singing softly: 'Farewell and adieu to you fair Spanish ladies, Farewell and adieu to you ladies of Spain...'

Remember *Jaws*? Quint, Brody and Hooper sitting round the table swapping scars? You've got him, Ian McGregor Bruce.

The bridge was one hundred and twenty metres above the Zambezi, that's almost four hundred feet in old money.

We rode up to the bridge I was planning to leap from and initially all we could see was the spray lifting like smoke. Riding closer we saw them, the Victoria Falls, millions of gallons of water, the largest in the world. They were magnificent, incredible; the river was wide and flat as it approached a great fault in the land and the water just fell away. It cascaded in great curtains into raging rapids. That was where I would plummet, and it had seemed like such a good idea back in London.

I wasn't the only one jumping; we'd hooked up with the support crew and Jimmy Simak was up for it as well. We stood together beside the little metal platform that only had three sides. Jimmy told me he'd never felt so nervous in his life.

I wasn't exactly a bundle of beans myself. I stepped on to the platform first and this smiling Zambian was chatting to me.

'How many times have you jumped before?'

'Never.'

'So this is your first time.' He laid a palm on my shoulder. 'Let's hope it's not your last then, eh?'

With that he strapped my legs together, attached a rather frayed-looking cable and stepped away. 'All yours,' he said. 'We'll count to five and you go.'

I glanced at the other side of the platform, the bridge side, the safe side where Ewan and Eve were looking on.

'I feel sick just watching,' Ewan called.

'Thanks, mate. That makes me feel a whole lot better.' I hopped to the edge of the platform.

'Big jump,' I said.

'We'll count you down,' the Zambian told me. 'Say goodbye to your wife. Five, four, three, two...'

'Aagghhhh!' I was gone, a huge leap, a swallow dive, well, falling very fast anyway. The first few seconds it was 'Holy Shit!' but then 'Wow! Fantastic.'

There was a lot of pressure on my face but God, I'd do that again.

Charley bungee jumps over the falls. As if riding all the way through Africa wasn't enough of a challenge!

EWAN: Jimmy made his jump, plummeting to certain death before being hauled up by the cable and bouncing around like a yo-yo above the rapids of the Zambezi. Not for me, boys – but hats off to you, that's for sure.

In the morning we were heading for the river crossing into Botswana and Eve was leaving for home. God, I was going to miss her – seven days was nowhere near enough.

When the moment came there were a few tears. Actually there were more than a few.

'Two weeks,' I told her. 'Two weeks and I'll see you again. I love you. Kiss the children for me.'

'I will. I love you too.' And then she was gone.

I woke to the sound of footsteps.

Lying there, I tried to work out who it was and how close the footsteps were to the tent. I thought it might be one of the others going for a pee. We were just over the border in Botswana, and had decided to camp together for the first night.

Rolling over I closed my eyes to go back to sleep.

Then I heard it again, slow, heavy footsteps. My heart began to thump. I stared into the darkness. I heard something crunch in the undergrowth, the swish of branches and a deep rumbling sound.

Jesus Christ. Elephants.

We'd seen their droppings when we arrived, but they were old and there was no sign that any had passed through for days. They were back now, though, and my tent was right in the middle of their path.

I had to get out – they'd never see the tent, just trample it with me inside. I unzipped the flysheet and stuck my head out. Quickly I grabbed a pair of shoes.

'Ewan!' A sharp hiss. 'Ewan!' It was our fixer Rick. Grabbing some jeans I pulled them on.

'Ewan! Come over here. You need to get out of the way of the elephants.'

'I'm coming, Rick,' trying to call in a whisper that was loud enough for him to hear. 'I'm coming.'

I was about to set off through the darkness when I realised my mosquito door was open. Better zip it up, I don't want to be bitten by mosquitoes after I've been trampled by elephants.

In the morning I found their tracks, massive footprints. They were oval shaped and three times the size of my hand. I found where they'd snapped off some leafy branches, then came across an indentation in the dust where one elephant had snuffled something with his trunk. He'd been twenty feet from my tent.

The roads were getting easier to ride at this point. Still had to watch out for the wildlife, though . . .

We were taking a couple of days off at a lodge in the Okavango and we flew up in a small plane, a mass of fresh water and islands below us, delta country, swamp and grasslands, with pockets of solid ground. It was an amazing sight.

We were met by our guide, a man who called himself 'Doctor'. He wore a leather bush hat and drove a jeep with high-lift suspension and raised seats in the back. There was a spotter's chair fixed to the front wing so his mate could locate the wildlife. Doctor gave us some quick dos and don'ts as regards life in the Okavango then we were off, bouncing along a marsh road right through the swamp itself, water rushing by.

Our destination was Mapula Lodge, a ranch style house with adjoining cabins built right on the edge of the lagoon with an amazing, view of the waterland that made up the Okavango Delta.

CHARLEY: We saw an elephant almost immediately, a solitary bull wading through the shallows. He was a massive animal with enormous ears and half-length tusks that showed the wear and tear of his years. He turned his rear end on us, then wandered into the trees.

We spotted giraffes and jackals, and a small herd of wildebeest that galloped over to take a look at us. I'd never seen these animals in the flesh. They were big and athletic with massive heads. Black manes ran the length of their spines and with their heads down they bellowed at us like cattle.

253

Then we were off to find a pack of African wild hunting dogs – the most endangered species in southern Africa. That notwithstanding, Doctor told us, they were by far the most successful hunters in the dog family, wolves included. They hunted as a unit to bring down impala – which they devoured very quickly so larger predators like hyenas and leopards didn't have time to steal it from them.

Doctor took us to the den where the pack was rearing pups. The adults were a tawny brown colour with massive ears and dappling across their hides. The pups were darker with white socks and they bumbled around hunting for scraps while the alpha female looked on.

While most of the pack would join together to hunt the impala, babysitters would stay behind and look after the young. The other dogs would bring food back and regurgitate it for them.

We saw baboons crossing the road carrying babies on their backs and we saw kudu: large antelopes with huge ears that walked with their heads jerking.

Back at Mapula we climbed into log curraghs; canoes that our guides poled across the lagoon. Now we were at eye-level with the grass, the water, the wildlife. Doctor pointed out flowers that floated on the surface – day lilies he called them: they closed their petals at night. We saw fish eagles just above the trees, then moments later and very close we heard the grunt of hippos.

We got close enough to stand up in the canoe and see half a dozen of the massive beasts lolling below the surface. This was the most dangerous animal in Africa and we were on the water with them.

EWAN: I had another elephant moment back at the lodge. I took a walk and found a couple among the trees. I was filming myself with my back to them, doing my best impression of David Attenborough. This one big guy was getting closer and closer as I was muttering away. I suddenly realised just how close.

Turning round I looked up at him and him down at me. He must have been about ten feet at the shoulder with huge ears and massive tusks. Suddenly he came at me – he flapped his ears and tossed his head, trumpeting at me. I took off at a run. I could hear him coming. Oh, shit! And I thought the other night I was in trouble.

Suddenly Doctor appeared on the path, lifted his arms to make himself big and shouted at the elephant. It stopped, considered him for a moment then half-charged. By now I was on the veranda looking back. Doctor stood his ground and shouted again. The elephant made another false charge and then finally wheeled away.

Right, I thought, now I know what to do. If he makes a false charge, stand your ground and yell at him. You'll be fine, Ewan. Unless of course it's a real charge. Then you'll be dead.

That night we went out again and came across a large-spotted hyena with her pup. She was very close and unafraid of the light, nursing her pup and watching us with relative disinterest with her long and large head, and massive bone-crushing jaws. Hyenas are not to be messed with – a bite that helps rot their food and more jaw pressure per square inch than any other land mammal.

A porcupine scuttled across in front us. It got trapped in the headlights, thought 'oh shit', and hid behind a bush about a quarter of its size.

We can see you!

Can you? Really? All right. It scuttled off into the night.

We heard a weird call ring out from some distance away. Doctor swivelled round in the driver's seat. 'That's buffalo,' he said. 'A distress call.'

We were off, racing into the swamplands. He thought the buffalo might have been attacked by lions and this was our chance to see them. We drove for two hours trying to find where the call had come from and pretty quickly we were surrounded by hundreds of bawling, snorting buffalo.

We hunted for the kill but didn't find it.

Just a couple of days off and yet it felt like a week. I was refreshed enough to get back on the bike and ride 120 kilometres of shitty sand road.

CHARLEY: It was incredible to realise that after such a mammoth journey we only had ten days to go. My mood fluctuated between tremendous excitement about seeing Olly, Doone and Kinvara, and pangs of sadness that I'd no longer be throwing my leg over the saddle every morning. The thing about travelling like this is you get so used to it, so excited about what each day might bring, that you can't quite contemplate stopping.

22

NAMIBIA TO SOUTH AFRICA

A MOTORCYCLE DIARY

EWAN: Only a handful of days more to go and the trip would be over. I was feeling torn, dying to see my kids and yet not wanting the wheels to stop rolling.

We were entering Namibia now and had only one more border to cross. I glanced at Charley as he packed away his passport. Two women wearing huge colourful dresses were watching us. They had headdresses I hadn't seen before – like headscarves only with a piece of cloth rolled horizontally at the front that looked like a pair of horns.

It was here that we bumped into Johannes, a young guy from South Africa who had been on the road for a few months, meandering through Uganda and Kenya. He didn't gauge his trip by distance or time: it would take as long as it took. I asked him when he'd be home and he said he didn't know. He still had two books to read yet, and a story to write.

I spoke to a Namibian policeman who was really interested in the bikes. 'Do you get many motorcycles coming this way?'

He shook his head. 'Almost never.' And with that he waved us over the border.

Charley pulled the obligatory wheelie and this time I popped one of my own. The police closed the iron gates behind us and we were into the desert, an 'elephant crossing' sign beside the road.

CHARLEY: We were heading for the Skeleton Coast. The land was flat, the road a faint ribbon of gravel with nothing but sand and cactus drifting to the horizon. Namibia was an enormous country, vast and empty, and we seemed to be the only people on the road.

It was good gravel, dusty and hard, not that it mattered now because since Kenya Ewan had proved he could cope with anything. One of the real pleasures of the trip had been watching him getting better and better. Now he was really confident and I could see how much he was enjoying it. God, I'd loved these roads. I'd miss them when this was over.

That night we camped in a huge landscape of baked sand and cactus, and weird looking quiver trees that were all trunk with just a canopy of short branches that stuck up like feathered arrows.

We were into the desert now with the wind cutting across plains that were arid and dusty. The road was edged with dry yellow grass and quiver trees. We crossed bridges spanning waterless riverbeds and climbed into shallow black hills where the sand turned grey. Volcanic rock jutted on all sides, sharp as razors, the landscape almost lunar. Coming down again, we were gliding into basins where the roads were red dirt.

We rode across the desert all the way to the sea.

EWAN: Parking the bikes we sat for a few minutes and I thought, my God, that's the Atlantic – the infamous Skeleton Coast. This was the region the bushmen called 'The Land God Made in Anger' and Portuguese sailors referred to as 'The Gates of Hell'.

I told Charley. 'From the Road of Bones to the Gates of Hell – do you think there's something in that?'

'Something about us you mean?' He laughed. 'I don't know.' He gave me a hug. 'It's been great riding with you, Ewan.'

'You too, Charley.'

Even near the end of the journey, Ewan still found putting up the tent pretty exhausting.

We shook hands.

'What do you reckon,' I said. 'Shall we do it again?'

'I'm up for it. I think I might have another appointment with the Dakar first, though.'

I nodded. I looked out to sea where the wind was howling and rollers broke against the beach.

'They named this place for all the ships that have gone down,' I said. 'There are serious rocks out there, ships used to plough into them in the fog. The sailors that made it ashore starved, mostly.'

'Hence the skeletons,' he said.

We camped by a quiver tree under a full moon and got one of our better fires going. We wrapped up against the cold, ate boil-in-the-bag and began to reminisce.

The following morning we were riding south. Once we left these roads in Namibia that was it, tarmac all the way to Cape Town, and I was quite choked. The enormity of it all was beginning to come home to me – how it had been put together, how because of Russ and Dave, Charley and I were able to ride through Africa without worrying about logistics, border crossings, paperwork. It enabled us to really be touched by the country, uncluttered, our hearts and minds open. If people were then moved by what they read or saw on TV it was because we'd been touched, humbled by the experience.

We made it!

CHARLEY: Seventy miles from the South African border Ewan got a puncture and his bike started to fishtail. The rear tyre was almost flat. There was a hole big enough to require most of a tube of glue and two plugs. We weren't sure if it would hold but got it pumped up and made it to the border. Our last crossing on two wheels – I couldn't quite believe it.

The immigration office was next to a covered bridge that looked like something from *Sleepy Hollow*. We had our passports stamped for the final time, shook hands and got back on the bikes.

I pulled my last border wheelie, the biggest of the trip so far. Then we were in South Africa and the next stop was the lodge and Olly, Doone and Kinvara. Yeehaw!

We would have covered almost fifteen thousand miles by the time we finished, a convoy of riders following us into Cape Town. I'd miss my bike, my tent, my sleeping bag. I'd miss the African skies and talking to my family on the phone while watching the most wonderful sunsets. I'd miss riding with Ewan.

That night we stayed at a small motel where there was only one other guest. We got chatting and discovered he worked in adult education, training the teachers who taught the adults in the poorer areas of the Western Cape. He told us that much had changed in South Africa since the days of apartheid but there were still pockets of racism. The real divide between the people, however, was economic.

He couldn't quite believe that we'd ridden all the way through Africa. He said that many South Africans didn't travel the continent. They'd been told – taught in some cases – that Africa really was a dark continent full of violence and murder. It was the same story we'd heard from the scaremongers back in Britain. Apparently, when South Africans went on holiday it was usually to Europe or America, rarely their own continent. It's crazy the things people are told.

The truth is, Africa's no Mecca for machete wielding mercenaries, it's a continent full of people who just want normal everyday things like a home and somewhere for their children to go to school. In all the time I'd been here I'd not felt threatened once. I realised then how lucky Ewan and I had been to stumble into Russ and Dave; they'd put this whole thing together and because of that we were allowed to ride across Africa and hopefully we'd learned something along the way.

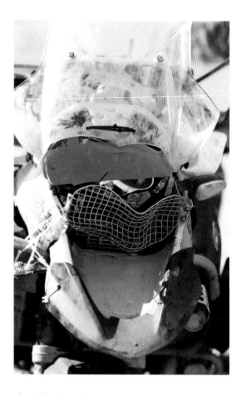

We were up before it got light. It was winter now, and cold and we had three hundred and forty miles to go. Ewan told me he didn't want the trip to end. He told me he'd miss hunting out a campsite and lighting a fire. He'd miss geep and elephants, and camels on the road.

He was concerned about his back tyre, though. The plugs had held so far but now we were in civilisation he thought he ought to get the tyre patched from the inside. We stopped for petrol and the guy serving told us there was a tyre place just up the road. Ewan went ahead while I filled mine and Claudio's bikes.

Paying the guy at the petrol station, I headed into town, not quite sure where Ewan had gone. I was messing about now, speeding up and hitting the back brake, sending the bike into a slide. The hard stuff was over, the adventure of it all, and I was relaxed and dossing around with stoppies and wheelies. Spotting the tyre garage off a slip road, I locked the back wheel and put the bike into a deliberate skid.

The next thing I knew Claudio hit me and slid past, the bike on its side and him whacking his head off the tarmac. His bike slithered down the road, glass shattering and sparks flying. I pulled up and jumped off.

Thankfully I saw him get up. He looked dazed and angry. Shit, I thought. Shit, shit.

'Claudio, are you all right?'

'Yes, I think so.'

'Man, that was a big one.'

'Fucking hell, Charley, you just hit the brakes! I was going to hit you and I had to swerve and that was it.'

'I had no idea you were so close. The last time I saw you, you were miles back.'

'You left me at the petrol station, I had to catch up.'

'Oh, man, I'm sorry.' I hugged him. 'Are you all right? God, I'm so sorry. I was dossing around, having fun, locking the back end. I'm sorry, Claudio, it was all my fault.'

'It's all right,' he said. 'It's OK.' He looked at his bike, lying on its side with the beak broken and headlight shattered.

I noticed the oil radiator was buckled.

The worst fall of the whole journey came just before we reached Cape Town: Claudio's bike was definitely worse for wear after an accidental collision with Charley's.

Ewan was alongside now. He'd heard the unmistakeably hideous sound of a bike sliding down the road. 'Fuck,' he said. 'What happened?'

'My fault,' I admitted.

EWAN: Claudio seemed more angry than anything else, but he'd come down hard on his right hand side and the lack of any pain was probably the adrenalin working. The oil radiator was bent back but it hadn't fractured and the bike was rideable. It was the old story: the last five minutes of any trip are the most dangerous – that's when complacency can set in and accidents happen.

Metaphorically we were five minutes from home now and this was by far the worst spill any of us had taken.

I got my tyre patched and we were back on the road. Not for long, though; Claudio's radiator burst, spraying oil everywhere. Claudio was really pissed off; all this way and now he couldn't ride his puppy into Cape Town.

Or maybe he could.

Between us we rearranged the gear on the back of the fixer's truck and loaded Claudio's bike. Getting on the phone, we arranged for the parts we needed to be brought to the lodge so we could get the bike fixed in time for Claudio to ride to Cape Town.

I checked my mirrors as we pulled away.

Eve was in Kenya now with my daughters and I was going to fly up to join them as soon as all the press stuff was over. My mum and dad had flown out to South Africa and they would be at the lodge to meet us, along with Charley's family.

Forty minutes out we were wet, cold and it was pitch black. We weren't sure where the rest of the team were so we tried calling various mobile phones, but nobody was answering except my mum. I told her we thought we were about forty miles away and we'd be there shortly.

It was all very strange, slightly surreal, but then I think that's how it is for anyone who's covered this amount of miles.

We'd left the desert behind, the dirt roads, the scrub and sand, the wildlife. But for some reason I thought of Ethiopia and the market town of Bati. I could picture this young boy who'd showed me around. There was something about him that seemed to sum up the trip for me. I hadn't known it then but in a way he personified the experience: yes, I'd been a guy on a motorbike and no doubt I would give him some money, which I did. But for the couple of hours we were there, there was a bond between us. For me these trips are about the people. People make up the places, without them the landscape is beautiful but empty.

We made it to the lodge and that was the second little ending of the trip. My mum and dad were there with the rest of the crew and it was great to see them. We met Paul and Keith, the two guys who'd paid so much to ride with us into Cape Town. The money was going to Riders for Health and it was those visits that had been some of the most memorable and moving of the whole trip.

The work of the Riders for Health clinic and its health workers on dirt bikes had been hugely inspiring. I thought about Scotland, CHAS and the people we'd been privileged to meet at Robin House. I thought about UNICEF and the mine-affected children in Zelambassa. I could see the village in Kenya where twenty-two children had been massacred. I could hear Daniel's voice, a child soldier in Uganda. All at once the memories began to flow. I could see Bulwer Street on the night we decided to do another trip; the Royal Geographical Society; the workshop at Avonmore Road. I recalled the moment when my bike arrived and the Friday back in February when I hit that pedestrian and broke my leg.

We'd done it. It was coming to an end, but we'd done it. Only I didn't want it to end. Right then I would happily have turned my bike around and ridden back.

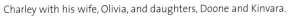
Charley with his wife, Olivia, and daughters, Doone and Kinvara.

CHARLEY: Finally we got to the lodge and there they were: my wife, my daughters. I hadn't got my helmet off and Olly had her arms wrapped round my neck; Doone and Kinvara were hugging me. At last I did get the helmet off and kissed Olly, kissed the girls.

'Hello, my darlings.'

We hugged and kissed. I held Olly for all I was worth and in that moment I realised just how much I'd missed her and just how lost a soul I'd be without her. I picked up Doone and Kinvara, kissed them. I couldn't stop holding them.

And there was Ewan's mum. 'Hello, Charley,' she said.

'Hello, Carol. Told you I'd bring him back safe.'

Ewan was hugging Olly and my daughters, Russ's mum and dad were there, as well as Emily his daughter. It really was a welcome party.

The following morning we left the lodge for Cape Agulhas and the final stage of our journey; a great convoy of bikes, the support vehicles and our families. On perfect black tarmac, Ewan and I rode side by side, taking in the coast where the sea was green and the sand flat and white. And then finally, beautifully, wonderfully, we came to a last bit of dirt road that would take us to the point.

We'd made it. Cape Agulhas, the most southerly tip of Africa and we'd started at the most northerly tip of Scotland. Almost journey's end. We were standing at the foot of the world with the Indian Ocean on one side and the Atlantic on the other.

'We did it, Ewan,' I said.

'We did. You and me, mate. To the bottom of Africa, fifteen thousand miles.'

'Hell of a trip,' I said.

'But good, I mean really, really good. Maybe we should do it again sometime. What do you think?'

'I'm up for riding back right now.'

'You know what, mate? So am I.'

EWAN: Hundreds of people had turned out to ride with us. Lachlan from BMW South Africa had done a tremendous job organising bikes for our friends and the people who'd helped us put this thing together. It was brilliant, the perfect finale. The trip had been Charley and I for sure, but it was more than that – it was our families, friends, it was the fans of Long Way Round, it was Dai Jones and Jim Foster, it was Jimmy Simak and Claudio. And not just them: it was everyone back in the office, everyone who'd seen us off that first morning. It was wonderful to honour all that effort now with so many motorcycles.

People crowded round us, a sea of faces and lines and lines of motorcycles. My dad was there and I caught his eye. He smiled at me. I glanced at Charley, at Russ and David as they got back on the bikes they'd ridden from the lodge this morning. This whole thing was about motorcycles and it was fitting that the team that put Long Way Down on the map would ride the last leg together.

We fired up the engines and pulled away from Cape Agulhas. We were on the blacktop: Charley alongside me, I reached across and grabbed his hand.

The noise of the engines was drowned suddenly by another, larger, meatier engine altogether: a helicopter. It dipped above us, a cameraman hanging out the door. I thought of Colin, my brother and former Tornado pilot; he'd arranged a fly-by to launch the trip at Castle Mey. Perfect, I thought, a tornado to begin and a chopper to finish. Kicking down a gear, I tucked in and cracked the throttle.

And finally there was Cape Town cradled in a valley – the sprawl of skyscrapers, suburbs and shanties dwarfed by the might of Table Mountain. I realised this was a dream, a childhood dream: motorbikes and meeting people in the most extraordinary places.

Yet it feels more like the beginning of a journey than the end of one.

CHARLEY: On the outskirts we pulled over and draped the Scottish flag Ewan's nephew had given us across the back of Ewan's bike. I could hear him singing 'O Flower of Scotland' and then we were on the last leg, cruising through the streets to the Arabella Sheraton.

I thought about a final wheelie but strangely, perhaps, I was more reflective. The enormity of what we'd been able to achieve began to sweep over me, brought home I think by the little bit of gravel we'd ridden to get to the very tip of the continent at Cape Agulhas. I was suddenly humbled, a little bit of dirt where we stood on the pegs and stuck our elbows out. I thought of the Sudan, Ethiopia, Kenya, Zambia, Tanzania: all those gnarly, muddy, sandy, potholed roads. It occurred to me that ten years from now those roads would be gone, buried for all time under tarmac. The Africa Ewan and I had ridden through would be changed forever.

Finally we pulled up outside the hotel. I slowed down, winding back the gas and stepping down through the gears for the last time.

Ewan took his helmet off and worked a hand through his hair. 'Charley,' he said. 'Thanks, mate; it was a pleasure riding with you.'

We shook hands, southern Africa style, then embraced Ewan-and-Charley style. 'You too, mate,' I said, 'you too.'

Appendix A

ROUTE

Countries	Locations	Date	Km	Miles	Cumulative
UK	John OGroats – Crieff	12th May	472.0	295.0	295.0
	Crieff – Scotland/England border – Holy Island	13th	310.0	193.8	488.8
	Holy Island – Silverstone	14th	535.0	334.4	823.1
	Silverstone – London	15th	117.0	73.1	896.3
France	London – England/France border – Rimes	16th	478.0	298.8	1,195.0
Italy	Rimes – Dijon – France/Italy border Just East of Mont Blanc tunnel near Courmayeur	17th	697.0	435.6	1,630.6
	East of Mont Blanc tunnel – Lake Como – Camp site north Fidenza/Parma	18th	446.0	278.8	1,909.4
	Camp site – Siena – Rome	19th	517.0	323.1	2,232.5
	Rome – Amalfi Coast – Pompei.	20th	372.3	232.7	2,465.2
Sicily	Pompei – ferry to Sicily – Palermo	21st	710.0	443.8	2,908.9
	Palermo – Trapani	22nd	109.0	68.1	2,977.1
Tunisia	Trapani – Sicily/Tunisia border by ferry – Tunis	23rd	0.0		2,977.1
	Tunis – Sfax	24th	284.0	177.5	3,154.6
	Sfax – Matmata – Medenine – 40 km west of Ben Gardane	25th	271.0	169.4	3,323.9
Libya	Camp – Ben Gardane – Tunisia/Libya border – Tripoli	26th	246.0	153.8	3,477.7
	Tripoli – Leptis Magna – Surt	27th	465.0	290.6	3,768.3
	Surt – Tobruk	28th	810.0	506.3	4,274.6
Egypt	Tobruk – Libya/Egypt border crossing – Marsa Matrouh	29th	377.0	235.6	4,510.2
	Marsa Matrouh – Alexandria – Cairo/Giza	30th	503.0	314.4	4,824.6
	Cairo – Suez – Luxor	31st	778.0	486.3	5,310.8
	Luxor – Aswan	1st June	222.0	138.8	5,449.6
	Flight from Aswan – Nairobi for Riders for Health visit.	2nd	0.0		5,449.6
	Flight from Nairobi – Aswan	3rd	0.0		5,449.6
Sudan	Aswan – Egypt/Sudan border – Wadi Halfa (ferry)	4th	0.0		5,449.6
	Wadi Halfa	5th	0.0		5,449.6
	Wadi Halfa – Camp in Desert near Kosha	6th	142.0	88.8	5,538.3
	Kosha – Argo	7th	198.0	123.8	5,662.1
	Argo – Dongola – Mulwad	8th	108.0	67.5	5,729.6
	Mulwad – Khartoum	9th	501.0	313.1	6,042.7
	Khartoum – Qallabat	10th	561.0	350.6	6,393.3
Ethiopia	Sudan/Ethiopopia border – Shehedi	11th	30.0	18.8	6,412.1
	Shehedi – Gondar – near Simien National Park	12th	238.0	148.8	6,560.8
	Simien NP – Adi Arkay	13th	74.0	46.3	6,607.1
	Adi Arkay – Aksum – Adrigat	14th	215.0	134.4	6,741.4
	Adigrat – Day trip to Zalembessa with UNICEF – Adigrat	15th	0.0		6,741.4
	Adigrat – Mekele – Adisho	16th	172.0	107.5	6,848.9
	Adisho – Kombolcha	17th	252.0	157.5	7,006.4
	Kombolcha – Addis	18th	336.0	210.0	7,216.4
	Addis Ababa	19th	0.0		7,216.4
	Addis Ababa	20th	0.0		7,216.4
	Addis Ababa	21st	0.0		7,216.4
	Addis Ababa – Langano	22nd	215.0	134.4	7,350.8
	Langano – Yirga Alem	23rd	149.0	93.1	7,443.9
Kenya	Yirga Alem – Kenya/Ethiopia border – Moyale	24th	448.0	280.0	7,723.9
	Moyale – Walda	25th	149.0	93.1	7,817.1
	Walda – Marsabit	26th	74.3	46.4	7,863.5
	Marsabit – Lewa	27th	276.0	172.5	8,036.0
	Lewa – Nakuru	28th	215.2	134.5	8,170.5
	Nakuru – Lake Naivasha	29th	89.3	55.8	8,226.3

Countries	Locations	Date	Km	Miles	Cumulative
Uganda	Naivasha – Kenya/Uganda border – Mbale	30th	445.0	278.1	8,504.4
	Mbale – Jinja – Kampala	1st July	232.3	145.2	8,649.6
	Kampala fly to Gulu for UNICEF project	2nd	0.0	0.0	8,649.6
	Gulu, fly back to Kampala	3rd	0.0	0.0	8,649.6
	Kampala – Fort Portal – Near Kasese	4th	389.0	243.1	8,892.8
Rwanda	Near Kasese – Uganda/Rwanda border – Volcano National Park.	5th	408.3	255.2	9,147.9
	Gorilla tracking	6th	0.0		9,147.9
	Volcano NP – Musanze – Kigali	7th	119.0	74.4	9,222.3
	driving in hills around Kigali	8th	217.4	135.9	9,358.2
Tanzania	Kigali – Rusumu – Rwanda/Tanzania border – Ntumaga	9th	299.0	186.9	9,545.1
	Ntumaga – Kibondo – Kasulu – Uvinza – Bush camp near Kaloma	10th	323.2	202.0	9,747.1
	Kaloma – Katavi National Park	11th	227.8	142.4	9,889.4
	Katavi Rest Day	12th	3.5	2.2	9,891.6
	Camp – Sumbawanga – Camp 100 km before Tunduma	13th	282.0	176.3	10,067.9
Malawi	Tunduma – Mbeya – Tanzania/Malawi border – Chilumba	14th	483.6	302.3	10,370.1
	Chilumba – Livingstonia – Rumphi – Nkhata bay – Chinteche	15th	269.7	168.6	10,538.7
	Chinteche – Salima – Senga Bay	16th	311.2	194.5	10,733.2
	Senga Bay – Lilongwe	17th	127.1	79.4	10,812.6
Zambia	Lilongwe – Mchingi – Malawi/Zambia border – Chipata	18th	220.5	137.8	10,950.4
	Chipata – Petuake – Kachalola – Camp by Luangwa river 60km from Kachalola	19th	399.1	249.4	11,199.9
	Camp by river – Lusaka – Choma	20th	493.4	308.4	11,508.3
	Choma – Livingstone	21st	211.0	131.9	11,640.1
Botswana	Livingstone – Zambia/Botswana border – Camped just north of Nata.	22nd	320.0	200.0	11,840.2
	Camp – Maun – camped in the delta in Mapula	23rd	377.0	235.6	12,075.8
	Day in Swamps	24th	0.0		12,075.8
	Maun – Nokaneng – camp in bush on way to border.	25th	235.0	146.9	12,222.7
Namibia	Camp – Botswana/Namibia border – Tsumkwe	26th	218.8	136.8	12,359.4
	Tsumkwe – Grootfontein – Otjiwarongo – Omaruru	27th	690.0	431.3	12,790.7
	Omaruru – Uis – Mile 108 – Henties bay	28th	401.3	250.8	13,041.5
	Henties Bay – Swakopmund – Bloedkoppie area, Namib Naukluft Park	29th	189.9	118.7	13,160.2
	Bloedkoppie area, Namib Naukluft Park – Sossusvlei	30th	245.3	153.3	13,313.5
	Sossusvlei – Keetmanshoop	31st	493.0	308.1	13,621.6
South Africa	Keetmanshoop – Namibia/South Africa border – Bitterfontein	1st August	628.9	393.1	14,014.7
	Bitterfontein – Gansbaai	2nd	541.1	338.2	14,352.8
	Gansbaai	3rd	0.0		14,352.8
	Gansbaai – Cape Agulhas – Cape town	4th	394.2	246.4	14,599.2
TOTAL			23,358.7		14,599.2

TOTAL MILEAGE INCLUDING FERRIES AND FLIGHTS 19197.95

Appendix B

EQUIPMENT

Navigation and Communications

Mobile communication and navigation all in one device: Nokia 6110 Navigator (8). Satellite phones and BGANs supplied by AST.

List of Tools – all supplied by MacTools

12" Adjustable wrench, 3/8"–1/4" adapter, Brass drift punch, 16oz ball peen hammer, 3/8" Super steel centre punch, 5/16" Combination wrench 12pt, 11/32" Combination wrench 12pt, KS2 Combo wrench standard (3/8", 7/16", 1/2", 9/16", 5/8", 11/16", 3/4", 13/16", 7/8", 15/16" and 1"), 3/4" Super steel chisel, 6/12/24v Circuit tester, 3/8" x 7/16" Flare nut wrench, 1/2" x 9/16" Flare nut wrench, 5/8" x 11/16" Flare nut wrench, 25bld Univ Mstr feeler gage st, Bend-a-light Pro-new, 3/8" x 7/16" Halfmoon wrench, 1/2" x 9/16" Halfmoon wrench, Punch & chisel holder, 5/8" x 16" Lady foot pry bar, 8" Mill bastard file/CG, 1pt, 1"–1/4" Telescoping mirror, 1/4" Ratchet 5", Macinists pocket rule 6", Telescopic pocket power magnet, KS2 Combo wrench metric 10mm, 5/16" Standard socket 12pt, KS2 Combo wrench metric 11mm, 11/32" Standard socket 12pt, KS2 Combo wrench metric 12mm, 3/8" Standard socket 12pt, KS2 Combo wrench metric 13mm, KS2 Combo wrench metric 14mm, KS2 Combo wrench metric, KS2 Combo wrench metric 16mm, 16" Speed HDL 1/4" DR, KS2 Combo wrench metric 17mm, KS2 Combo wrench metric 18mm, KS2 Combo wrench metric 19mm, 1/4" DR, 2" Knurled extension, Metric Long Combo Wrench 21mm/12pt, Metric Long Combo Wrench 22mm/12pt, 1/4" DR Universal joint, 10" Big champ pliers, 7 3/4" Curved diagonal pliers, 6" Slip joint pliers, 1/4" DR, 6" Knurled extension, 1/4" DR Spin handle/comfort grip, 3/16", Standard socket 12pt, 7mm Comb wrench 12 pt, 7/32" Standard socket 12pt, 8mm Comb wrench 12 pt, 1/4" Standard socket 12pt, 9mm Comb wrench 12 pt, 9/32" Standard socket 12pt, #1" x 3" Phillips Bolster/CG/Red, #3" x 6" Phillips Bolster/CG/Red, 5/16" x 6" Std tip Bolster/CG/Red, 5/16" x 8" Std tip/CG/RED, 1–1/2" Flexible putty knife, 1/4" x 1.5" Std stubby, 3/16" Long S/S pin punch, Foam profile, 8" Needle nose pliers w/cutter, #2 x 1.5" Phillips stubby, 8" Round bastard file/CG, 5/16" S/S roll pin punch, 1/8" S/S roll pin punch, 1/4" S/S roll pin punch, Ratcheting screwdriver (2), 8" Square bastard file/CG, 9pc Metric hex key set with case, 13pc Speed hex key w/cset, 1/8" S/S starter punch, Black frame clear safety spec, 3/4"–2" ADJ hook spanner wrench, Pitch gauge bolt & thread, 3/8" x 7/16" Wrench, Open-ended wrench 9/16" x 1/2", Open-ended wrench 5/8" x 3/4", Digital mulitmeter, 10" C-JAW Vise-Grip+R w/cutter, 7" Straight jaw Vise-Grip+R, 10" Ratchet 1/2" drive, 10" Extension, 1/2" Socket 12pt, 18" Flex handle w/comfort grip, 9/16" Socket 12pt, 2" Extension, 5/8" Socket 12pt, 11/16" Socket 12pt, 3/4" Socket 12pt, 13/16" Socket 12pt, 7/8" Socket 12pt, 1/2" Universal joint, 15/16" Socket 12pt, 1" Socket 12pt, 5" Extension, 12mm Socket 6pt, 13mm Socket 6pt, 14mm Socket 6pt, 15mm Socket 6pt, 16mm Socket 6pt, 17mm Socket 6pt, 18mm Socket 6pt, 19mm Socket 6pt, 21mm Socket 6pt, 22mm Socket 6pt, 24mm Socket 6pt, 3/8" Ratchet, 8" Flex handle, 3/8" Socket 12pt, 7/16" Socket 12pt, 10mm Socket 12pt, 11mm Socket 12pt, 3" Knurled extension, Universal joint, 6" Knurled extension, slotted bit (2), #1 Phillips ACR bit, #2 Phillips ACR bit, Metric pitch gauge, MacTools battery charger – 12v up to 100AH.

BMW spares

Emergency cylinder head kit (3), Rocker cover (2), Gasket (8), Bolt (4), O ring (1), Plugs (4), Coils (4), Clutch Field (1), Lever (2), F Pads (6), R Pads (3), Brake fluid (1), Headlight bulb (1), Tail bulb (1), Bracket hand (9), Bracket (9), Extra tank bags (3), Front and Rear discs (spare discs for bike) (2), Tyres (16), Extra keys (4), BMW front shock absorbers (2), Rear BMW shock absorbers (2).

Nissan spares

Air filter (2), Pollen filter (2), Sets of wiper blades (2), Dampers with bushes (4), Fuel filters (4), Alternator (1), Set of engine bells (1), Engine injectors (2), Car set light bulbs (2), Tin plastic Metal (2), Tin rad weld (2), Engine oil (1), Engine coolant (1), hi-lift jack (1).

Camping Equipment supplied by Touratech

Touratech – Ortlieb roll closing q packsack (8), Touratech – Ortlieb TRACK day pack (8), Touratech – Ortlieb premium travel mat (8), Powerstretch Gloves (8), Haglofs Barrier Jacket (L) (6), Haglofs Barrier Jacket (XL) (2), Anadir Sweater (XL) (2), Anadir Sweater (L) (6), Fram Pants L (6), Fram Pants (XL) (2), Roll Closing Q Packsack (XL) (8), Haglofs Bum Bag (8), Eagle Creek Undercover Security Wallet (8), Pack-It Sport (black) (2), Pack-It Sport (cherry red) (2), Pack-It Sport (neptune) (2), Cascade Pack Shower (3), Ortlieb T Pack (5), PackTowl (XL) blue (8), Pocket Soap (8), Hammock (2), Clothesline (2), Mutha Hubba Tent (8), Touratech Tent Bag (8), Marmot Sawtooth sleeping bag (2), Yeti Energizer 750 (6), eVent compressing packsack (L) (8), Travel pillow (8), Ortlieb Premium mat (8), Walkstool (8), Outdoor Mosquito net (8), MSR Dragonfly cooking stove (2), MSR fuel bottle (4), Ortlieb Collapsible dishes (2), Titanium Multi Compact

(2), Snow peak titanium thermal tumbler (10), Stainless steel plate large (10), Stainless steel plate (10), Salt-n-pepper shaker (4), Curry-n-herbs shaker (4), Titanium cutlery (10), Nalgene loop top bottles (8), Nalgene wide mouth bottles (8), Drink powder 'Rouge' (20), Letherman charge Ti (8), Active thermos flask (8), Micropur water purifier (8), Ortlieb waterbags (8), MasterLED torch (8), Princeton Tec Aurora (8), Strap It Motorbike Adjustable (10), ROK All purpose Adjustable (10), ROK All purpose Flat 30cm (4), ROK All purpose Flat 60cm (4), ROK All purpose Flat 90cm (4), ROK All purpose Flat 150cm (4), Strap It Motorbike Flat 300mm (4), Strap It Motorbike Flat 450mm (4), Strap It Motorbike Flat 600mm (4), Strap It Motorbike Flat 750mm (4), Neck Brace (3), Mountain equipment pneumo stuffsack 5 ltr (1), Mountain equipment pneumo stuffsack 15 ltr (1), Mountain equipment pneumo stuffsack 25 ltr (1), Mountain equipment pneumo stuffsack 50 ltr (1), Haglofs Bum Bag Watatait (1), Pack-It Quick Trip toiletries bag (1), Packet Soap (8), Pack-It Quick Trip toiletries bag (1), Packet Soap (1), Yeti Sunrizer 800 (1), Touratech Aluminium Camping seat (3), Snow Peak GIGA Power WG (1), Trangia Spirit Stove Ultralight HA (1), Nova Multi Fuel Burner for Trangia cooker (1), Snow Peak Titanium Multi Compact cooking set (1), Snow Peak titanium thermal tumbler (1), Lexan Plate flat 25cm (1), Nalgene loop-top bottles, Lexan (1), Katadyn COMBI water filter (4), Airchamp tubeless tyre puncture repair kit (4), Tyre pressure gauge (2), eVent compression bag Medium (1), ProLite 3 Regular Therm-a-rest (1), Touratech Mess Kit (1), Zega Case (black) (1), Auxiliary Bag (1), Snow Peak GIGA Power WG (1), Twin burner stove – petrol (1), Honda generator- EU10i (1), Wayfarer Boil in the bag foods: spicy vegetable rigatoni, meatballs pasta in tomato sauce, chocolate pudding, chicken pasta and mushroom, sausage casserole, beef stew, beans & bacon in tomato sauce (various), Space Cases: various sizes (4), Mosquito repellent (30), Deet (30), Howling Moon 2-man roof tent (3).

Clothing

Powerstretch Gloves (8), Haglofs Barrier Jacket Large (6), Haglofs Barrier Jacket (XL) (2), Anadir Sweater (XL) (2), Anadir Sweater (L) (6), Fram Pants (L) (6), Fram Pants (XL) (2), Touratech Haglofs Fleece jackets (8), Belstaff customized jackets (2), Belstaff customized trousers (2), LWD beanies (8), Rain jackets (8), LWD Personalised T-shirts (60), Underwear, Socks, Shorts, Hiking boots, KSB Sport Sandals, Jeans, Cotton shirts, UNICEF LWD Buffs, LWD logo hats (8), BMW Rallye2 Suit (1), Zip-off cargo pants.

Video/Photography equipment

Sony Z1 Camcorder (1), Sony HVR-V1e HDV video camera (3), Sony HRV-A1e HDV Video camera (3), Sony HDR-HC7E handycam (2), Sony HC96 Dv Cameras (6), Sony V1e hard drive (1), Sony MDRV150 headphones (1), V1e camera batteries (7), A1e battery charger – AC5Q950 (4), A1e battery charger (6), A1e batteries (12), Sennheisser boom mic and cable (1), V1e battery charger (4), Sennheisser EK100 radio mic(transmitter & reciever)set (2), Sony top mic (1), Swit S-2000 light (4), Audio splitter cable (1), Rode NTG-1 external mics with softie (3), Travel adaptor plug (8), Century Optics Wide Angle lens (1), Leica Dlux 3 digital camera (6), Velbon tripod (1), Sennheisser headphones (1), Sennheisser boom mic + cable (1), Hyperlight and charger (1), Sony top mic (1), Audio splitter cable (1), RSA1U-A1 raincovers (1), DV-970L lithium battery (3), Uniross AA/AAA battery charger + mains lead (1), Uniross AA rechargable batteries (16), Uniross AAA rechargable batteries (8), Canon DSR 450 zoom lens (1), RSPD170 raincovers (1), Sony toplight (3), Travel plug (10), Century Optics Wide Angle lens (1), Canon 30D SLR camera (1), Canon speedlight 430EX (1), RSA1U-A1 raincovers (1), Century Optics Wide Angle lens (1), Nikon SLR D200 (1), Plaubell Makina 670 stills camera (1), RSA1U-A1 raincovers (1), 1500GB raid 5 storage device with foam protection (2), Additional set of raid 5 drives and caddies (4), Pelicase for 10 drives case-1520 (2), PC PCI-X SATA card for AVID (1), PCMCIA SATA adaptor for PC Laptop (3), Panasonic Toughbook 51 Core Duo 1.66Ghz 4Gb Ram 100Gb HD- laptops (3), Additional batteries for Panasonic Toughbook (3), Additional power supply to Toughbook (2), Pelicase for toughbook and HDV deck (3), AVID express pro software (1), Sony HVR-M15 deck (3), Sony VCL-HG0862K (0.8x Wide Conversion Lens for V1) (1), Sony HVR-DR60 Hard Disk Recorder (60GB) (1), Tripod GITZO Traveller (G0041587) MANFROTTO (701 RC2) (2), Sony Charger AC-SQ950 with car charger (for two 7.2V Lithium M batteries) (1), Hawk-Woods DV-MC2 Charger (for two 7.2 Lithim L batteries) (1), Hawk Woods DV970L DV link battery (15), Hawk Woods DV-RH1 (Sennheiser radio-mic holder) (3), Hawk Woods DV-CA12 Step-Up Adaptor (5), Sony Diversity URX-P1 receiver , +UTX-B1 transmitter (3), Sennheiser SK100Tx transmitter + EK100Rx receiver (2), Sankon tie mic (for Sennheiser radio mics) (6), Sankon tie mic (for radio mics) (4), Audio Technica tie mic (for radio mics) (4), Sony Gun Zoom Microphone ECM-HGZ1 (1), Rode directional mic NTG-1 + Rycote Softy (2), Headphone Sennheiser HD25SP (1), Sony AA+AAA charger (1), Uniross Sprint AA+AAA charger (1), Rechargable AA batteries (20), Rechargable AAA batteries (12), Surge Protection Multiple power socket (2), Leica HL-005 Batteries for Leica camera (12), Sonic helmet cameras and mics (6).

Picture credits

WITH THANKS TO:

Photographer	Page numbers
Julian Broad	1, 2-3, 4-5, (all) 7, 9, 10, 22, 42, 50, 59, 60, 74, 78-79, 104, 134, 136, (top) 139, 168, 170, (top) 186, (bottom right) 188, (bottom right) 189, 198, 202-203, 204, 209, 210, 214, 216, 222, 225, 226-227, 242, 258-259, 260, 262, 263, 264, 265, 266-267, 268-269, 270, 271, 272, 273, 288
Russ Malkin	32-33, 49, (bottom) 62, 65, 67, (bottom) 70, (bottom) 71, 73, 77, 88-89, 106, 110, 122, 143, 150, 161, 165, 171, (bottom right) 182, (bottom) 183, (top left) 187, (bottom) 187,
Rob McDougall	13, 21, 24-25, 26, 29, (all) 30,
Ewan McGregor	34, 40, 120, 145, 148, (bottom) 224,
David Nikon	39, 41, 44, 46, 47, 55, 56, 57, (top) 71, 81, 84, 87, 90-91, 93, 97, 101, (all) 102, (middle and bottom) 103, 107, 108-109, 111, 114, 117, 121, 123, 124, (all) 127, 132, 133, 135, (bottom) 139, 140, 141, 142, 146, 147, 152, 154, 155, (all) 157, 158-159, 160, 162, 166, 167, 174-175, 176, 178, (all) 179, 181, (top and bottom left) 182, (top) 183, (right) 183, 184, (bottom) 186, (top right) 187, (left) 188, (top) 188-189, (middle and bottom left) 189, (top and middle right) 189, 191, 193, (all) 196, (all) 197, 200, 201, 211, 212, (all) 217, 218, (top) 224, 228-229, (bottom) 230, 232, (all) 239, (all) 241, 244, (all) 245, 248-249, (bottom) 250, 252, (all) 253, 254, 255, (bottom) 257,
New Ollie	15, 20, 36, (all) 276, (all) 278, 279,
Claudio von Planta	52, (top) 62, 80, 130-131, 153, 156, 177, 195, (top) 230-231, (top) 250,
Jim Simak	45, 86, (top) 103, 112-113, 194, 215, 219, 221, 238, 247, (top) 257,
UNICEF	128, 205, (all) 206, 234,
Charley Boorman	275

SO WHAT NEXT?

When we got off our bikes in Cape Town at the end of Long Way Down, people started to ask 'So what next?', 'Will there be a Long Way Up?', 'Any more journeys planned?'. Well, we can now give an answer. There's definitely one more journey taking place and we're fully committed to make it happen. What is it? It's our journey to try and raise as much money as we can for UNICEF and children affected by HIV, poverty and conflict all over Africa. We're calling this journey 'The Long Way to Go' because whilst UNICEF is reaching millions of children across the continent already, we want to go all the way to help them in their mission to reach every single child, and that's no mean feat.

Having travelled across Africa on Long Way Down, it's been a privilege for us to work with UNICEF, meet children and hear first-hand about their lives. A lot of people ask us, 'Doesn't it get depressing hearing about these terrible things and seeing children living in difficult situations?' But the truth is, strangely, it doesn't. Because the children we have met on our travels are incredibly brave. They have hope. They have UNICEF and its partners, taking action to make their lives better. We've seen how it works with our own eyes: the education and opportunities that UNICEF gives children who have grown up knowing nothing but war, the simple miracle of preventing babies being born with HIV, the incredible care and love that UNICEF gives to children orphaned by AIDS. They have made a long lasting, incredible impression on us.

Crossing Africa we realised the enormity of what UNICEF has set out to do. Without any funding from the UN, they need money urgently to reach every child. So please join us on this new journey. You don't even need a bike. Just dig deep in your pockets and give something to UNICEF – however much it is – to help make the world a better place for every child. We've seen what a difference it can make.

www.unicef.org.uk

UNICEF is the leading children's organisation, reaching children in more than 190 countries around the world. We work with families, local communities, partner organisations and governments to help every child realise their full potential. We support children by providing health care, nutrition and education. We protect children affected by crisis including war, natural disasters and HIV.

UNICEF is not funded by the UN. Instead we rely on voluntary donations to fund our work for children worldwide. We need help from people like you in order to continue supporting and protecting children from the effects of poverty, conflict and disasters. Even the smallest donations can make a huge difference to a child who has nothing.

If you live in the UK, you can help UNICEF by donating or by taking part in a fundraising event or by lending your voice to our campaigns. Please go online and do something to help the world's children at **www.unicef.org.uk/longwaydown**.

Alternatively, you can donate by calling 0800 037 9797 and quoting 'Long Way Down' or send a cheque to:

UNICEF
Long Way Down
Freepost CL885
Billericay
CM12 OBR
United Kingdom

If you are outside the UK there are still many ways to support UNICEF, *please visit* **www.supportunicef.org** to find out more.

Children's Hospice Association Scotland
Sharing the Caring

Children's Hospice Association Scotland, CHAS is a Scottish charity committed to providing hospice services for children with life limiting conditions and their families. Sadly, hundreds of Scottish families are facing the fact that their child will not live to be an adult.

CHAS runs the only children's hospices in Scotland, Rachel House in Kinross and Robin House in Balloch, as well as an at home service called Rachel House at Home for families in the Highlands. CHAS provides respite care, practical help and emotional support to the whole family, from the day they are referred until the death of their child and beyond.

These services are free of charge to families but it costs CHAS £5 million each year to run Rachel House, Robin House and the Rachel House at Home service.

If you would like any more information about CHAS, please visit our website at **www.chas.org.uk** or contact us at the address and telephone number shown below.

CHAS
Canal Court
42 Craiglockhart Avenue
Edinburgh
EH14 1LT

Tel: 0131 444 1900
Scottish charity number SC019724

www.riders.org

Motorcycles saving lives

10.8 million people are now receiving regular healthcare, sometimes for the first time in their lives.

Billions of dollars are spent each year to produce drugs and vaccines to prevent men, women and children dying needlessly from easily preventable and curable diseases. But they fail to reach the people who so desperately need them. This isolation from health care resources is due to the fact that the population of Africa live far from towns and major centres, the distances are vast and the best roads are little better than dirt-tracks. Even when vehicles are available, they quickly break down if no one has the expertise or resources to maintain them.

So Riders for Health addresses that vital missing link. We make sure, with our highly trained local teams, that motorcycles and other vehicles used in the delivery of health care withstand the harsh conditions and keep running day in, day out. We work in Zimbabwe, the Gambia, Nigeria, Kenya and Lesotho, training health care workers in safe riding and preventative vehicle maintenance.

Charley and Ewan's experiences on the ride gave them a first hand understanding of the distances and difficulties involved in riding in Africa. These are the same difficulties that the health care workers face every day.

To find out more about the work of Riders for Health or to find out about how to make a donation, please visit **www.riders.org**.

Acknowledgements

Olivia, Doone, Kinvara and the whole Boorman clan
Eve, Clara, Esther, Jamyan and our family

David Alexanian and Russ Malkin.

Lisa Benton, Sarah Blackett, Ollie Blackwell, Julian Broad, Kelly Bushell, Mike Clark-Hall, Dave Depares, Joanna Ford, Jim Foster, Jeff Gulvin, Daryl Higgins, Corin Holmes, Dai Jones, Robert Kirby, Asia Mackay-Trotter, Liz Mercer, Claudio von Planta, Andy Ryder, Robin Shek, Jimmy Simak and Lucy Trujillo.

Antonia Hodgson, Caroline Hogg, Marie Hrynczak, David Kent, Tamsin Kitson, Alison Lindsay, Duncan Spilling and everyone at Little, Brown Book Group and Janet James.

Special thanks to:
Arai: Wendy Hearn
AST: Chris Wood and Tracey Harris
Belstaff: Manuele Malenotti and Michele Malenotti
BMW: Steve Bellars, Pieter De Waal, Lachlan Harris, Tony Jakeman, Juergen Korzer
Buff: Julian Peppit, Ignasi Rojas
Cafédirect: Sylvie Barr
Castle of Mey: Jeremy Mainwaring Burton, James Murray, Jackie Phillipson
Eurotunnel: John Keefe
Explore: Paul Bondsfield, Peter Eshelby, Ashley Toft
MacTools: Adrian O'Nion
Media Insurance: Boyd Harvey
Michelin: Paul Cordle
Nissan: John Parslow, Bob Neville at RJN, Russell Joyce at Motormode
Nokia: Amooti Binaisa, Jenny Williams
Sonic: David Bryan, Wayne Schreier, Liam Thornton
Standford maps
Starwood: Amalie Craig, Rob Kucera, Robert Scott
Total: Iain Cracknell
Touratech: Herbert Schwarz
Virgin Atlantic: Richard Branson, Paul Charles, Bill Gosbee
Visit Scotland: Karin Finlay, Liz Ware

CHAS: everyone at Rachel House and Robin House, and Barbara Osbourne
Riders for Health: Andrea Coleman, Barry Coleman, Jennie Goodman
Unicef: Sarah Epstein, Alison Tilbe, Wendy Zych

All stills photos by Julian Broad taken on Canon digital cameras.